JIM DOWNS

APPRECIATING
A$$ETS

An Australian guide to creating

wealth – and keeping it!

Published by Jim Downs
Real Estate Investors Network
GPO Box 160 Sydney NSW 2000
tel: 1800 001 003
fax: 1800 002 303
net: www.rein.com.au

ISBN 0-646-42025-9

Researched, edited and co-written by
Renata Whitewood

Project management by
Danny Vandine, Upside Down Productions
net: www.upsidedown.com.au

Cover design and *Appreciating Assets* logo design by
David Horsburgh

Layout and typesetting by
Scripts & Graphics

Illustrations by Agung Cahyadi

Printed in Australia 2002

Disclaimer: Because every investor's needs and financial situations are
different, the ideas in this book are intended as an educational guide
only. Proper consultation with your financial adviser should be
undertaken before implementing any investment strategies.

Acknowledgements

To my life-partner, Jenny Robbie, thank you for your help and encouragement, to my daughter, Julia, for your inspiration and to my mother, Gloria, for your support and love.

Thanks to my editor Renata Whitewood, who collaborated with me on the writing of this book and turned my words and ideas into print; to Danny Vandine for managing this project and to David Horsburgh for design and layout.

To the team at REIN, thank you for all your effort and dedication and, of course, to all REIN clients, past and present, without whom this book would not exist.

CONTENTS

JIM DOWNS
APPRECIATING
A$$ETS

HOW TO APPRECIATE ASSETS!

The author of *'The Richest Man In Babylon'* George S. Clason describes wealth as "a child born of knowledge and persistent purpose". In a nutshell, this is the basic creed of all financially intelligent people. Appreciating Assets is aimed at increasing the financial intelligence of its readers. Financial intelligence is not something we are born with, nor something we learn in school. One day, I hope, it will be included in the school curriculum. Until then, books such as this one have an important role in both creating and steering financial intelligence. Without this financial intelligence, wealth becomes a slippery customer that evades the grasp of many hardworking, well-meaning people.

The foundations for both Real Estate Investors Network (REIN) and for this book began life at the end of the World War II, before I was born. My father returned from the war and was given a grant of twenty pounds with which he bought seven acres in Belrose in New South Wales in 1946. He married and began his family. In 1966 he sold this land and found himself with enough money to retire at forty-three years of age. He bought a dairy farm on the North Coast of New South Wales.

He sold again a few years later and retired to Ballina with my mother. He used his time and money to "help the kids", as he put it. My sister had a rebuild of her home and he helped my brother complete his home. He spent a few years with me building a 50-foot steel-hull sailing yacht. He was a fabulous father. He was in the right place at the right time twice in his life, holding real estate assets worth substantially more than he paid for them. The money he realised from the sales of these assets moved our lives from working class to middle class.

I went on to study electrical engineering. During that time one of the bosses I was working for came to me and shook my hand. He said,

"Jim, congratulations, mate. If you work really hard, in 40 years you'll be just like me!"

I looked at him and it hit me. Here was my epiphany! I had to sit down because I knew he was right. This was the point at which I started to work out who I wanted to be and what I wanted to do with my life. So the next thing I did was quit! I then lived the cliché of the 60s. I bought a 'Kombi' van and drove around Australia to 'find myself'!

In 1974 I ended up in Townsville in Northern Queensland just before Christmas. On Christmas Day I turned on the radio and listened to the news. Cyclone Tracy had hit Darwin. Out of that destruction came an idea. I got on a plane to Darwin and started a painting and decorating company. I had rarely picked up a paintbrush in my life, but, within six weeks, I had contracts to paint 440 houses. By my 24th birthday I had made enough to sail my boat around the Barrier Reef with no destination in mind.

At 28 I got married, so life changed again. I lost my boat in a cyclone (how ironic!) and was faced with life on dry land in Sydney, with about $40,000 in the bank. I decided to put this money towards buying

I bought a 'Kombi' van and drove around Australia to 'find myself'!

an investment property. I was going to buy a block of land on Paradise Island in Surfers Paradise, Queensland for $64,000, but my father-in-law, a wealthy businessman, advised me to go into business instead, and I listened to him.

Two years later the real estate agent rang me and told me the same block of land had just been sold for $180,000. In that two years I had worked day and night in my small business for a profit of $40,000 once I had sold the business. Something didn't add up! Sometimes free advice can be very costly! However, I did learn some valuable lessons that would help in the future.

My first property investment was in Newtown and cost me $11,000. Later I bought properties in Paddington for prices ranging from $32,000 to $176,000. By 1984 I owned four properties. I renovated them and put tenants in them. I had little idea about negative gearing or tax deductions. I did it the hard way!

By 1988 I was running a successful company in Sydney. At this point I could have retired from business and lived happily on the income from my investment properties by my 40th birthday. I worked incredibly hard. I travelled, I trained, I ran seminars. In the meantime my wife ran off with an accountant!

One expensive settlement later, I was in the position of having to start again! So I did. I ran another franchise network and built up my income again. In 1995 I was earning a comfortable six figure income with credit cards and lifestyle to match. I sat down to work out how and where I was going and it dawned on me. I was an idiot! I had nothing to show for all this work except some expensive toys and decorations.

I thought back to a conversation I had with a developer in North Sydney in the early 90s. I had said to him that I wanted to buy properties again, but I did not have the 10 per cent deposits. I also wanted a lot of clauses in the sales contracts and a discounted price! His reaction, not surprisingly, was one of mirth! He then added that, if I could bring him 30 buyers, he would do it. So the conversation bore fruit four years after the seed was planted. Why buy one at a time, when there was more benefit to buyers and seller from buying in larger numbers. I worked on this idea and realised that the purchasers would need me as much as I needed them. This new business plan was based on a symbiotic relationship.

I began by running seminars. No one came to the first seminars! All the people I had employed drifted off, thinking I had lost it! Finally people came and I made my first investor purchase in 1996 using this new

3

format, which paid for the next seminar. Real Estate Investors Network grew from there.

Napoleon Hill, in his classic book *'Think and Grow Rich'* says,

"One sound idea is all that is needed to achieve success."

This investment system has evolved from one good idea and has benefited over a thousand investors by providing them with a financially secure and comfortable future. My partner Jenny and I invest in most of the property that REIN invests in. This is the main part of my plan for a future I would want to live in. Many of my employees have done the same. We are working together and, through this solidarity of numbers we can achieve more than an individual working alone.

Moments of truth

If you were to take the story I have outlined above and consider its 'watershed' moments, they would be, in chronological order:

- **Using money to buy assets.** When my father was given his grant of £20 on returning from the World War II, he bought something that would increase in value, land. He bought something that would put money in his pocket, an asset.

- **Using one asset to generate another.** My father sold his first purchase 20 years later and used the money to buy a bigger asset. He could have held onto it and borrowed on its equity, but his decision paid off. He was able to retire at 43 and then sold the second property for enough money to retire on.

- **Realising that working hard and earning a good income for 40 years is not enough to be wealthy.** When I was confronted by the fact that, after 40 years of hard work, I would not be wealthy and independent, my motivation to find another way was increased. My desire and my ambition were brought to the forefront of my mind and I had to look at my life from a different frame of reference. From this change in the frame I had to build up a new picture of how my life would be.

- **Recognising an opportunity and acting on it immediately**

is necessary for financial progress. Cyclone Tracy was a disaster. Out of this disaster came opportunity. The opportunity was only recognised because I was looking for it. Had I not got to that stage in my life, I would have missed the opportunity to create something worthwhile and positive out of chaos.

- **One good idea is all that is needed to generate wealth.** The idea to start a painting and decorating company in Darwin was not radical, nor could I call it a stroke of genius. It was simply the right idea at the right time and in the right place. It did not take Einstein to work out what people were going to need in Darwin in early 1975. It was not an act of charity either. People paid for a fast, efficient service and were happy with the results. The business flourished through word of mouth, because we were doing a good job at the right price and we were doing it quicker than others. I even created extra long rollers to speed up the process! The idea helped people who were trying to get back to normal in their lives and also helped my team of workers and me financially.

- **Free advice can be extremely expensive.** When my father-in-law advised me to go into business for myself, it was not bad advice. It was, however, advice that did not fit in with my original plans. I allowed his advice to turn me away from my original intention of buying land on Paradise Island. I listened to a man who knew little about property investment and was swayed into putting the money into starting a small business. More fool me! I lost out to the tune of over $80,000. This was some years ago, so we are talking nearly $200,000 in today's money. That is an expensive mistake!

- **Using income to increase assets is the quickest way to build wealth.** Buying one house, renovating, putting in a tenant and using the income generated to buy the next one meant I could continue to build on my assets. My extra income went into more properties, rather than an increase in my spending and my consumerism. Whatever my favoured investment vehicle, as long as I used the income generated from it to buy further investments, it would have continued to build greater assets for me.

- **Keeping an eye on the Big Picture is necessary.** By the 'Big Picture' I mean the international, national and domestic picture. Whilst wars, government financial policies and natural disasters may have a bad effect (in the short term) on investments, particularly in volatile areas such as shares, the domestic front can also create havoc. This chaos is possibly longer-lasting than anything a military junta, fundamentalist terrorist group or a drought can throw at you! A marriage breakdown, serious ill-ness or the loss of employment can be more detrimental to your financial health than anything on the world stage. Some of the potential damage can be minimised or overridden by sensible planning and insurance, such as income protection or death and trauma cover. If you can minimise any of your risks, DO IT!

However, as I found to my extreme cost, some of what life hits you with cannot be planned for, insured against or predicted. In which case, if your motivation is strong enough and your ambition is solid then you have no choice but to start again and learn from what has happened. I did it, and I'm not Superman, just an ordinary man with strong desires and ambition to match!

• **You can't be wealthy if you keep spending it!** Taking a long, hard look at your spending habits is painful but has to be done. To get anywhere with wealth creation, you will need to monitor what money comes in and what money goes out of your financial system. Then you will need to adjust the balance so that more comes in than goes out. After years of living in comfort and style, I realised I had little in the way of income-generating assets. When I calculated how much I had spent in one year I was aghast! This spurred me on to the next part of my road to wealth.

• **Planning is part of the process.** I set myself a goal and then followed this with some serious and detailed planning. Through this plan-ning, the goal is made believable and attainable. In my case I had a set figure in mind and then worked out a way to reach it.

• **With persistence anything is possible.** Have you ever noticed tree roots pushing up through concrete? Annoying to the person who laid the concrete, but what a marvel of persistence and single-minded dedication to one goal!

During the days, weeks and months when I put on seminars that no one came to, people drifted away from me and everyone around me was quite happy to write me off as a lost man fighting a lost cause. Regardless of what they thought and said about me, I was protected by my single-mindedness, my ambition, patience and a healthy ego. Without these qualities, all of which are parts of the quality we call persistence, I would have given up and allowed other people to label me as a failure.

Many people enjoy failure in others, because it makes them feel bet-ter about their own lack of success. Rather than emulate success, there are many unsuccessful people out there who will happily undermine and

known as the 'baby boomers'.

The 'baby boomers', born in the two decades following the Second World War, currently 40 to 55 years old, make up nearly a quarter of our total population. These people, when they retire, will cause the overall percentage of people in the workforce to drop, since they make up such a large proportion of the overall population.

With the oncoming retirement of the 'baby boomers', income tax revenue will fall even further. If the government does not encourage people to become self-funded retirees, it is faced with the impossible task of providing pensions for a rapidly growing sector of our society, the older Australian. Bear in mind that this will also put much more stress on an already over-burdened Medicare system, since older people, on average, need more costly and more extensive health care.

A report from the Australian Institute of Health and Welfare published in 1998 commented on this increase of stress on the already stretched health services.

"On average, older people tend to be higher users of health services. Compared to the rest of the population persons over 65 years have, per capita, health expenditure four times higher…"

The Australian Bureau of Statistics has projected that the percentage of people over sixty-five will rise from 12 per cent in 2001 to 27 per cent in 2031. The percentage of people over 85 will rise five times from 1 per cent in 2000 to 5 per cent in 2051. The average age of Australians in 2001 was 35.5 years. In 2031 it will be 42.2 years.

The Bureau's 1999 report on "Population Projections: Our ageing population" states that population ageing is a major focus of social and economic planners and policy makers throughout the developed world.

"Of particular concern is the anticipated increase in costs associated with the care and income support of a rapidly growing aged population, and how much Australians will be willing and/or able to pay. Much of recent government policy has focused on cost reduction as well as shifting costs and responsibility from the public sector to individuals, families, community groups and private business."

Where are we heading?

According to the United Nations Report on Ageing, published in 1998, 31 per cent of Japan's population is over 60. Japan is, as we know, facing the challenge of recession and its economy is suffering. One third of its population is under 60 and working. One third is too young to work. Another third retired. In other words, only one third of its population is in the workforce and paying tax. Australia is forecasted to have 27 per cent of its population over sixty by 2020. It doesn't take a crystal ball or amazing psychic powers to work out that we are approaching the same state as Japan.

As the working population in 1992 in Australia was probably at a peak, incomes were at their highest, tax was also filling government coffers and we began a wave of spending. This will probably last until 2010, with the majority of the baby-boomers retiring. After that, spending will drop, the economy will be heading for recession and the government will have no choice but to reduce its spending, along with the rest of us. This is a very good reason to aim for financial independence now, whilst there is still time to generate it.

What about superannuation?

The compulsory superannuation schemes set up over the last few years are an attempt to take some pressure off the state and to create self-funded retirees, but will it be enough? Certainly for the younger people amongst us who will be in the workforce for many years to come, superannuation will support many of them once they retire. But for those who are in their 40s and 50s, the future looks very different. Research carried out by the Association of Superannuation Funds of Australia (ASFA) in 2000 found that over 70 per cent of the people interviewed by ASFA did not expect that superannuation would be enough to give them financial independence on retiring. Just under 80 per cent of the people interviewed thought they would need at least half of their gross income before retirement to live on after retirement. Half of these respondents added that they would really like 80 per cent of their pre-retirement gross income.

Unfortunately many people will find that, when they retire, their super funds will not enable them to live in comfort and freedom from financial worry and stress. Many will be living on incomes of less than a quarter of their pre-retirement incomes.

The current government of Australia is concerned that many people within 10 years of retirement will not have enough superannuation put aside to create a comfortable retirement. The retraining and job-search assistance schemes currently funded by the government through its social welfare policies are attempts to get older people who have been made redundant or who have been forced to retire early back into the work-force to top up their superannuation savings. It is probably a case of too little, too late.

It is a sad and unnecessary fact that according to the Australian Bureau of Statistics 95 per cent of Australians currently in retirement live on less than $25,000 a year. It is even more remarkable and depressing that eighty per cent live on less than $12,000 a year. As I write this (2002), the current full pension for a single person is $205.25 a week. For couples it is $342.60 a week.

Only approximately 1.5 per cent of today's retirees have retirement income of more than $40,000 a year. Will you be one of these people when you retire? Or will you be one of those 95 per cent struggling to make ends meet?

Where are we heading?

If you choose to do something about your financial future, you must be aware of the time factor. The time to do it is NOW. Start early enough and time works for you. Leave it for a few more years and you will find that time is no longer your ally, it has become your enemy. The two most common causes for financial hardship in retirement are starting a financial plan too late in life or never starting one at all.

Wealth is a decision. Wealth is a choice. Choose to do nothing and you are choosing to be poor.

Imagine that you are around 40 years old. You have $30,000 in your super fund and own a house in Sydney's northern suburbs. Actually, you own most of it, there is still $90,000 owing on the mortgage. The house's current value is $400,000. In 12 year's time, at the age of 52, imagine you have paid off the mortgage. The house is now completely yours. You decide you want to retire at 55. Let's say the house you live in is worth $800,000 when you reach 55 and your super fund is up to $300,000. Sounds good so far? Think about it.

At 55 you will no longer have an income. Your house, whilst a very nice house and all your own, does not bring in one cent of income. In fact it costs you money to maintain it. Your super (at an estimated 6 per cent per annum) will bring you approximately $18,000 a year. You will be one of the 95 per cent.

If you wish to do something about it, if you choose to be wealthier than the 95 per cent, read on.

What stops people investing?

Having ascertained that there is a real and compelling need to look to our financial futures and create self-sufficiency and financial independence for our retirement years, how can we explain why only five per cent of the Australian population is currently able to do this?

Is financial independence and comfort such a difficult goal to achieve? Does it need millions of dollars to start with? Does achieving this goal require a university education? The answers to these questions are, "No.", "No." and "No."

As many financial experts have already stated in their own seminars, lectures, interviews and books, it is not rocket science. It does not need a degree in economics, or, for that matter, any degree. Nor does it need a long and expensive series of seminars with the latest dynamic guru of the cult of self-development through colonic irrigation or strange yogic positions facing a mirror in a candle-lit room. We already have the ability to achieve this goal within us, if we choose to bring it out and use it.

If it is not the degree of difficulty that stands in our way, what does stand in our way? **To put it simply, we have not been taught the habits, the attitudes and the concepts of financial intelligence. Financial intelligence is the key to our creation of wealth, our development of wealth and our maintenance of wealth.**

No school or further education establishment in this country runs courses in it. Banks do not promote it. Governments do not promote it. This is one of the main reasons why 95 per cent of our population have not been able to gain the freedom of worry that financial independence brings and why millions of us live out our lives in financial discomfort and anxiety, needlessly.

The only way to create financial independence is to create assets. As we know, an asset is something that generates a passive income. Once managed competently, it gives us an income, with little or no effort on our part.

The cashflow of the financially intelligent

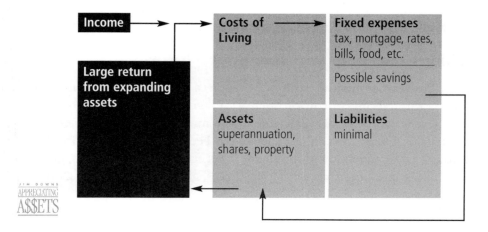

Compare this to the cashflow of the financially unintelligent.

The cashflow of the financially unintelligent

Here the income is used to generate liabilities in the form of loans for holidays or cars or money spent on new lounges, new kitchens or a spa bath. These liabilities will not earn money (unless you use the car for a hire car service or run cooking classes from the kitchen!). In fact, they will lose money from day one. They will depreciate in value, unlike assets,

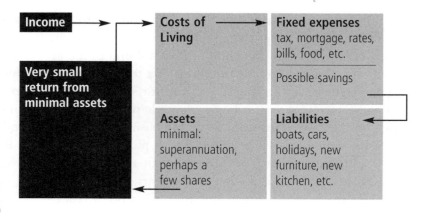

which appreciate in value.

The ability to create or acquire assets and to maximise their value can be hampered or destroyed by several bad habits or negative thinking patterns. Let's consider the main habits or fears that get in our way.

Things that help you stay poor

The fear of losing money. Firstly, let's consider the fear of losing money through investment or the fear of failure of an investment plan. This fear is very real and very large in the minds of the majority of Australians. Every adult in our society has been exposed to horror stories, through family, friends and the media, concerning market crashes, global instabilities and other miscellaneous slumps, gluts and doom and gloom predictions.

We are all aware that life in general can be a risky business. Does this mean that we wrap ourselves in cotton wool and stay in bed, not daring to venture out, in case a bus hits us? To the ordinary human being it means an acceptance that there is some risk and a policy of risk management in everyday living.

We look both ways before crossing a road. We insure ourselves against risks of theft and accident. We manage our everyday risks as best we can and analyse likelihoods of events, such as helicopters dropping in during dinner or freak tidal waves ruining our beach picnics, so that we can sleep at night.

Throughout the book I will be identifying techniques and effectiveness of risk management and, through these principles you will reach a clearer understanding of investing with confidence and common sense.

Another way to look at this is to reverse time! Imagine that we are discussing potential investments that you would like to make. Now I tell you, in the next 15 years, there will be a war in the Middle East, a stock market crash, a crash in the bond market, a slump in the property market, a crash of technology stocks, the threat of a technological breakdown, extreme terrorist acts in America, major unrest in some key Asian countries and economies, and, at home, a couple of major droughts, an earthquake on the eastern seaboard, some big bush fires and a few floods too!

What would be your reaction to such prophecies? My guess is that you would change your mind about investing because the risks were too great. Now look back at the last fifteen years. Seems familiar? All I have described as a possible future came from the past 15 years!

These events really happened. Now look at the investment market today. Business as usual. For the longer-term investor, three years plus, these global and domestic calamities register as glitches on the growth charts of various investments.

How wars have moved the Dow Jones Index

Event	Initial reaction★	1 month later	3 months later	6 months later
Pearl Harbour	-6.5%	3.8%	-2.9%	-9.6%
Korean War	-12.0%	9.1%	15.3%	19.2%
Cuban Missile Crisis	-9.4%	15.1%	21.3%	28.7%
US bombing of Cambodia	-14.4%	9.9%	20.3%	20.7%
US bombing of Libya	2.6%	-4.3%	-4.1%	-1.0%
Gulf War	-4.3%	17.0%	19.8%	18.7%

★Initial reaction in some cases was over days or weeks. Source: Ned Davis Research

The bombing of Pearl Harbour did have longer-lasting repercussions than the other conflicts. This event brought the Americans into the Second World War and the Dow Jones Index (the measuring rod of the health of America's stock market) reflected the concern of US involvement in such a global conflict. Of course, once the war was officially ended, the US economy rebounded and surpassed its previous levels. For those who held tight whilst the Dow Jones Index showed negative trends, the rewards were spectacular! Those who sold when the market was at its lowest, only to see the market rise to new highs a couple of years later, must have felt a little sick.

After the Gulf War in 1991, the Dow Jones Index fell by 4.3 per cent. After one month it had recovered and risen by 17 per cent. Six months after the initial fall, the Dow Jones Index was still up by 18.7 per cent. Six months after the Korean War was begun and six months after the initial bombing of Cambodia, the Dow Jones had risen by around 20 per cent. Six months after the Cuban Missile Crisis, it was up by nearly 30 per cent! (Source: Ned Davis Research).

If you are prepared to keep your finger off the panic button and hold onto your investments for the long term, the areas such as property investments, managed funds and fixed-rate investments such as bonds and cash have been shown to withstand a lot of battering. Shares (if that panic button is left alone) have generally resumed and increased their values, in spite of short-term falls, even when the falls have been quite dramatic.

In the wake of the terrorist bombings in New York and Washington on 11 September 2001, one of the most respected investment experts, 'guru' Warren Buffet, reassured investors he would not be selling his stocks. On the contrary, he was actually looking to buy! When the average shares-investor is faced with a drop in share values through such a disaster, their first instinct is to 'cut their losses' and sell, sell, sell!

To the financially intelligent shares-investor the drop in value will result in two courses of action. One will be to hold onto what they have already, knowing the market values will be back to where they started, or even higher within a matter of months. (History has shown us this pattern again and again.) The second course of action for the financially intelligent investor will be to buy selected shares. Since many panic-stricken people are selling at a loss, the share values will fall quickly before common sense and a return to stability prevails. The financially intelligent opportunity-seeker has bought at bargain prices and can now sit back and watch their new shares' value rise over the following months.

Bear in mind that the share market is the most volatile investment market and yet still has a pattern of maintaining growth over a period of years, despite wars and other catastrophes, (as proved by the events of the last 15 years). It would be logical to assume that refusing to invest because there might be unsettled times ahead of us is not a decision that a financially intelligent person would make.

> "The main cause of poverty
> or financial struggle is fear
> and ignorance, not the economy
> or the government or the rich"
>
> Robert T. Kiyosaki

Cynicism. Secondly, we need to look at the damage to our futures done by cynicism. Cynicism is created in our minds by a synthesis of fear, doubt and pessimism. It is an habitual response to input from the outside world and is common throughout every area of our society. But remember, it is a habit, and habits can be broken if the desire to do so is strong enough. Cynicism can be likened to having a permanent sneer tattooed across our brain. The real danger of cynicism lies in its diminishment of our capacity for joy, optimism, ambition and learning.

It erodes self-respect and, consequently, respect for others. It destroys self-confidence and creates a view of the world as a place when only bad things happen. Cynical minds choose only to see the negative side of anything and choose only to believe that everyone's motives are negative.

When it comes to destructive habits, some say cynicism causes more damage than smoking. It is also more expensive than smoking. Cynical minds can rarely recognise an opportunity for success, since they will immediately dress it up as an opportunity for failure or exploitation.

This strange habit is a protective one, it protects us by making us do nothing. Consequently we do not need to worry about failure, ridicule or risk. We do not need to worry because cynicism prevents us from doing anything we can worry about! Of course, it also prevents us from learning, loving, growing in knowledge, in experience and, of course, in wealth. This is why cynicism is so expensive a habit. It will, if allowed to, cost us our relationships, our capacity to trust and believe and our potential to develop mentally and emotionally. It will also cost us our health and our wealth.

One example of the effects of cynicism can be found in the story of Guglielmo Marconi. Marconi, as the pioneer and inventor of the 'wireless' radio system, won many prestigious honours, including being made a Knight of Italy and winning the Nobel Prize for physics.

Marconi was met, many times in the course of his career, with cynicism, scepticism and even mockery. In 1895 he began laboratory experiments, sending wireless signals over a distance of one and a half miles (2.4km), thus becoming the inventor of wireless telegraphy, at the age of 21. His friends were so concerned, when he announced he had discovered a principle through which he could send messages through the air, without the aid of wires, or other direct physical means of communication, that they suggested he be put into a psychiatric institute and given help!

A year later he had moved to England because of the lack of encouragement received in his homeland, Italy. He again found himself facing doubt and cynicism, but still managed to gain a patent for his system, financed by his cousin, Jameson Davies. Davies also helped to form the 'Wireless Telegraph and Signal Company', which, of course, went on to make millions of dollars for the inventor and his backers.

Despite yet more cynicism and doubt thrown into his path by a group of distinguished mathematicians who claimed the Earth's curvature would limit practical communications to 100-200 miles, Marconi succeeded in sending a message 2,100 miles (3,381km) from Poldhu in Cornwall to St John's in Newfoundland in 1901. This was just the start of a prodigious and distinguished career that led to the development of radio technology as we know it today.

What if he had listened to the cynics?

This is one example of many. Galileo, Copernicus, Leonardo da Vinci, Magellan, Columbus, Edison, Bell, Darwin and Einstein are a few more examples. Each of these great inventors, discoverers and creators of works of genius were faced with ridicule, doubt and cynicism. Luckily, for all of us, they kept faith with themselves and their visions.

Laziness. Laziness, or the habit of expending as little effort as possible in any given situation, comes from several causes. Some of these causes are lack of self-discipline, leading to lack of self-confidence, lack of ability to set and maintain goals for living, lack of enthusiasm, lack of imagination and lack of ambition.

Laziness creates the "I can't afford it" mentality, since to ask oneself the question, "How can I afford it?" takes effort in the asking and answering. Saying "I can't afford it" needs no thought, no effort and no action.

It creates a reluctance to work out a budget and then to implement it, since changing things takes more effort than keeping them as they are. It culminates in a reluctance to take responsibility for oneself and one's actions. This lack of responsibility leads people into a 'blaming' mentality. "It's not my fault, it's the government's fault, the employer's fault, my parents' fault." This gives rise to a sense of powerlessness, "So there's nothing I can do about it." This diminishes a person's sense of power and confidence and leads to stagnation and depression in all areas of life.

Arrogance. Arrogance is often the disguise of people with low self-esteem and little confidence. True confidence is quiet and open to change and learning. Arrogance is rigid and unyielding, therefore easy to shatter or break. Arrogance, whilst being extremely unpleasant to the people around it, is also a costly habit to live with. As with cynicism, it can damage relationships, friendships, careers, finances and opportunities for learning. To the arrogant, there is nothing they can learn, they know it all already! The way they do things is the right way, even if it doesn't work for them! Then, of course, it is someone else's fault, not theirs.

Unwillingness to learn, to develop new skills and to be flexible and open to change, whether it comes through fear, cynicism, laziness or arrogance, has the same effect on the individual. It damages their capacity for interactions with others, for moving forward and making progress with their lives and for taking responsibility for where they are heading and finding the best way to get there.

All these habits are dangerous and expensive.

The Consumer Society. We are all members of this abstract and diverse club we know as 'society'. We are all prey to the pressures society places on us, and there are many. One of the greatest pressures is to 'conform', to be like all the others and so 'fit in'. To 'stand out' takes courage and confidence. Resisting pressures put on us by society and its mouthpiece, the media, means expending effort and maintaining self-discipline.

Fitting in means to look the same, to live the same and to shop the same! Many of us choose to keep up with those Jones people. A few choose to outstrip them in shows of wealth and comfort. The financially intelligent cross them off their Christmas list and don't return their phone calls!

Watch any commercial channel on television and you will be sold a dream of a modern 'El Dorado', a mythical country of gold. Interest-free credit, personal loans, 'buy now, pay later', 'no deposit, no repayment for six months'. But, as the Spanish discovered on their arrival in South America a few hundred years ago, such an 'El Dorado' is an expensive exercise in fantasy, greed and futility that gives far, far less than it seems to promise and counts its costs in blood and human lives.

Our commercial media has deteriorated to the point where it is hard to work out which are the programs and which are the advertisements. Extensive practices of product placement, sponsorship and cross-promotion put huge pressure on us to put it on plastic, pay for it later, borrow the money, because we want it NOW! After all, everyone else has got one, haven't they?

The financially intelligent are good readers. They read all the small print and also read between the lines. They are disciplined and use credit wisely. They obey a simple rule.

They only borrow money to buy assets

The financially unintelligent borrow money to buy dining tables, cars, holidays, boats and home-entertainment units. These consumer items are not assets. These are items that will lose money as they get older. These items depreciate as soon as you have bought them and will continue to do so for the rest of their lives.

The financially intelligent know that assets gain money as they age. Assets put money in your pocket. Unless that car you want to buy is a rare vintage car that will increase in value as it ages and become rarer, it's losing you money as soon as you drive it out of the car yard and into the petrol station for fuel and oil. And it will keep losing you money, through depreciation, through costs of services, tune-ups, repairs, parts, registration, insurance and parking fees.

So the financially unintelligent, who succumb to the lure of immediate gratification and the 'image is everything' mentality, will rarely be able to save money or invest. If they are unable to save money by spending less than they earn, they have little or nothing to invest with. They lack the personal discipline and imagination to follow the steps for successful creation of assets. Those who choose to disregard their financial future through fear, cynicism, laziness or arrogance shape a future for themselves that will leave them powerless and dependent on the state and the good will of their family. **Ironically, those who ignore the future will have little future to ignore.**

The cash flow of the financially unintelligent

Let's look at cashflows again. As money comes in to the lives of the financially unintelligent, it flows out again. Unless it is taken away before the average person gets hold of it, as with the forced savings of superannuation, it will get spent on both necessary expenses, such as bills, mortgages and rates, and unnecessary items, such as loan repayments for holidays, clothes, jewellery, entertainment and other non-essentials. Nothing, or very little, gets saved and put into the purchasing of assets such as shares, property or cash management units, so there can be little or no return from assets. In the worst-case scenario, people spend more than they earn, so generating perpetual and escalating debt.

Question: How much closer have you moved to financial independence?

Answer: You haven't!

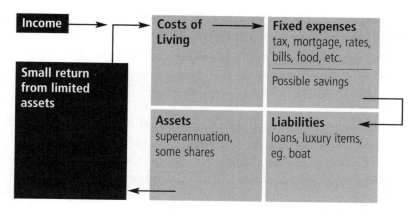

How many people repeat this pattern every day of every year of their lives? Unfortunately 95 per cent of us are currently trapped in this pattern because the priority is not **investment first.** We put our immediate desires before our future.

The cash flow of the financially intelligent

For those of us mindful of our future and wanting to be sure of creating a financial state of comfort and wealth, the pattern of cash flow is different. As our income comes in we firstly 'pay' ourselves by putting money aside to build up investment assets. I now put aside 30 per cent of my income automatically. When I started out, I put aside 10 per cent.

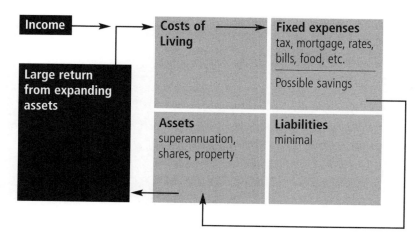

After we have looked after the assets, we pay the fixed costs and then we can use what is left over to either continue to increase our assets or to buy things with an easy conscience. We limit our liabilities, paying off loans, paying off credit cards, prioritising our future wealth over our immediate gratification.

Question: How much closer have you moved to financial independence?

Answer: You have moved to a position of being able to realise your financial independence for the future!

The financially intelligent will not sacrifice future comfort and wealth for immediate desires. Once the future has been taken care of, once the assets have been built up, then is the time for a little luxury and retail therapy.

CHAPTER 2

HOW DO WE MAKE INVESTMENT WORK?

"Riches do not respond to wishes. They respond only to definite plans, backed by definite desires, through constant persistence."

Napoleon Hill

Making the decision to create financial independence and stability in our lives and in our futures is obviously only the first step. What follows is learning which characteristics, which skills and which habits will serve us in this quest for wealth. We can begin by looking at it from the other side of the wealth fence and identifying the main reasons for failure to establish wealth and financial independence.

The main reasons for failure

The lack of a well-defined life plan. The need for a well defined, clear and specific plan of action in our lives is crucial to all areas of our life. For our purposes, this plan needs more than, "I want to be wealthy." It needs the answers to the following questions, "When? How much do I need? How will I do this? What will it take to achieve this?" It needs you to form goals and to work out how to reach these goals. If a football player runs onto the pitch and finds that someone has removed the goal posts, that player has nothing to aim for and no way of knowing when a goal has been scored.

Even with goals set in place, a clear plan of how you will achieve them is necessary. The successful football team will have a plan of the game in place before it runs onto the pitch. Imagine driving to a part of the city or country that you are not familiar with. If you have no map, you may wander around for hours or days, trying to find your destination. You may never find it and return home defeated. You may find it by sheer fluke, but the chances of this are slim to none.

A life led without plans is like a journey without a map. If you stick to the areas you have travelled in before, you will manage, but as soon as you are out of your familiar territory, you will get lost without a plan. With a plan you know where you are going, how to get there as quickly as possible and places you may want to visit on the way.

Lack of ambition. Ambition is a necessary quality to achieve your aim of financial independence. Without it, the hopes and wishes may be there, but nothing can actually be realised. Again it needs to be clearly defined. "I want more money" will not get you more money. A plan needs detail.

"I want to live independent of government pensions and have [this many] dollars per year derived from my investments to do this. I will need [this much] investment at this rate of capital growth and appreciation to create this level of income."

Ambition without a plan, or a plan without ambition is like a car with no petrol. It won't go very far!

"If you do not see great riches in your imagination, you will never see them in your bank balance"

Napoleon Hill

Insufficient financial information and knowledge. This is an area that confuses and scares many people. No, you do not have to go to college to acquire enough information to create a healthy investment plan. As I have already pointed out, the information you need is not generally taught in schools, but can be found in libraries, bookshops and newsagents in the form of books and magazines. The information can also be found through your computer at certain websites.

"Would you go to the breadmaker to enquire about the stars?"

George S Clason

Many people think their accountant will advise them on their financial futures and inform them of better ways to manage their money. They have the misguided belief that they must be doing the best they can because their accountant has not told them anything different. The accountant is employed to keep the figures, not to create them. The reason why your accountant does not offer financial advice is because an accountant is not qualified to do so – and is not being paid to do so.

If you are willing to pay for the service, the information can be presented to you by a qualified financial planner or adviser licensed with the Australian Securities and Investment Commission (ASIC). Remember that in most cases, free advice is worth what you pay for it! Check that a financial adviser or planner is a member of the Financial Planning Association of Australia Ltd (FPA). Also check that they are independent, ie. not linked to any particular bank, fund or scheme and will therefore be in a position to give impartial advice and recommendations.

Ask where they have their own investments. If they don't have any, I'd give them a miss. If they only favour shares in their own personal investment plans, it is likely that this particularity will be passed on to you. After all, if are asked to recommend a particular brand of coffee, it will most likely be the one you drink yourself.

Some advisers get a fee for placing clients in certain funds or investments. If you are not sure, ask. They must tell you if and how they will benefit by your choice of product, plan or fund. Ask where they get their information from and how up to date it is. If they start talking in terms of tithes and bushels of wheat, you have a fair idea that they are not exactly current in their knowledge of investment plans today!

Be clear in your own mind about what level of risk you are comfortable with, how long you want to invest for, how accessible the money needs to be and what outcomes you expect. The clearer you are, the better able the adviser is to serve you, rather than peddle whatever plan or product suits them. Ask them about complaints procedures and how complaints are managed.

What about your friends and family? They may have advice for you on financial matters that they are only too willing to pass on. But who would you ask for help if you have a problem with the wiring in your house – your brother, your father-in-law or your neighbour? Surely none of these unless one happens to be a qualified electrician. After all, electrical work needs a certain level of competence and experience. You want to get it right, or there could be dangerous consequences. So, when it comes to financial management, surely it makes sense to go to a qualified or experienced expert in the field. After all, you want to get this right too! The consequences of using the wrong person for the job are also dangerous!

Wherever you choose to access the information, be prepared to study it, analyse it and question its appropriateness to your situation. At the end of this book there are some suggestions for further reading and also the addresses of useful organisations and websites.

Lack of self-discipline. If I was to offer you a plate of broccoli or a slice of chocolate cake, which one do you think you'd choose? If you have spent your life so far choosing chocolate cake, you are not alone. Imagine that a distant relative has died and has left you an inheritance of $5,000. What would you do with it? Most people would be able to spend such a sum in less than a week. A new piece of furniture, a holiday, clothes, shoes, jewellery, a new computer, the latest in home-entertainment technology – decisions, decisions!

One thing most people would not do is invest it or use it to decrease debt. It's chocolate cake all the way! Oscar Wilde wrote that nothing succeeded like excess. For immediate gratification perhaps, but at the end of his life, Wilde found himself poor, sick, despised and imprisoned.

If you make the decision to choose wealth and financial independence in your life, self-discipline is going to be a necessary component of the successful achievement of this plan. There are no short cuts, no easy routes. This is why a clear and compelling plan is vital. If you can keep the end in mind, choosing the broccoli gets a little bit easier. Practise this choice often enough and it becomes a habit!

I am not saying you must never choose the chocolate cake. Life would be very dull if we lived as the Puritans did three hundred years ago, with absolute sobriety and no laughter (or whistling) allowed on Sundays! Going back to that imaginary $5,000 you could always invest or pay off debt with most of it and then spend a small part. That is to say, eat the broccoli first and then have a small piece of chocolate cake. With a well-shaped plan, the ambition to achieve it and the habit of self-discipline in place, you will find it easier to make correct choices and to weigh up future gains against immediate gratification.

Blaming others – the 'poor me' syndrome! Another key to success in any part of your life is to accept responsibility for your actions and their outcomes. Many poor people have a host of reasons for why they are poor. "My parents were poor, they never left me any money. My boss doesn't pay me enough. I can't save any money. It's hard enough to live on what we get now. The kids cost too much. I had to leave school to get a job, so I don't know how to invest."

Blaming parents, bosses, kids, families, governments and education systems does one thing for the blamer. It lets them off the hook. It makes them feel they are not responsible for their situation in life. It's not their fault. It also makes them feel powerless and resentful. It turns them into cynics and takes away their ability to hope and to think for themselves.

Many of the people I have had the pleasure in assisting through REIN inherited nothing or very little from their parents. Many are on incomes that fall a long way short of generous. Nearly all of them have two, three or more children and very few of them knew much about wealth creation and investment when we first met. One thing they all share is the acceptance of personal responsibility for their choices, their decisions, their actions and the outcomes of those decisions.

Procrastination. Procrastination, or the fine art of putting things off, is linked to a lack of self-discipline. It also ties in with the habit of blaming others. "I can't do this now, my wife/kid/brother/mother wants me to mow the lawn/go to the park/fix the dripping tap/feed the dog..." and any number of other plausible reasons for not doing what you are meant to be doing.

One way to prevent procrastination is to use your imagination! Create a mental picture of the outcomes of wealth creation or find a real image, a photograph or picture, and place it in a position in your house where you will see it every day. Having a picture of your goal in front of you is often all you need to create the momentum to get started. Another strategy is to take the task you are putting off and break it down into a series of smaller tasks. Dangle a carrot on a stick, if it helps. Promise yourself a small reward on the completion of the task or tasks. It could be anything, from a glass of wine and a good book or video once you have completed some paperwork or information gathering, to a long weekend in the mountains or at the beach once you have reached a certain stage in your investment plan.

The ability to maintain a clear plan of action in your mind and keep your ambition fuelled by picturing the outcomes of wealth creation and showing yourself appreciation of your progress will limit the damage done by the habit of procrastination. In other words, begin with the end in mind and work steadily towards it.

Lack of persistence. Without persistence, ambitions and plans dwindle very quickly into wishes and regrets. A lack of persistence will, ultimately, prevent the successful outcome of any plans you make. No matter how intelligent, talented or inspired you are, if you lack the persistence to see things through to their fruition, your plans and efforts will result in nothing. Persistence means keeping on, even when you are tired, bored or frustrated. A clear picture of your goals and the progress you have made so far will help to keep you motivated.

Read a book! Reading biographies and autobiographies of people who have struggled against the odds or in the face of adversity or criticism (and most of these life stories include struggle and overcoming adversity of one kind or another) can be one way to keep up your persistence. They are human. You are human. If they can do it, so can you.

Colonel Sanders, when he lost his income at 66 years of age, took one look at the amount of money he would get in his pension and went to work for himself. He travelled around the United States trying to sell his recipe for fried chicken. He got turned down 1,009 times before he got his first sale! From there he proceeded to become a millionaire at the age when most of us are playing golf and knitting for the grandchildren. Without persistence, Harlan Sanders would have been just another poor and miserable pensioner. Most people don't 'fail', they just give up. They are unable to recognise the opportunity failure can bring!

"Failure is the opportunity to begin again, more intelligently"
Henry Ford

Wanting "something for nothing" If you expect to receive without first giving, to gain without spending effort, to win without putting up a stake, you have the laws of nature against you! You cannot reap what you did not sow. Anything multiplied by nothing equals nothing. In the words of one-time US president, Roosevelt, "There is no such thing as a free lunch."

Waiting for a large sum of money to fall into your lap will not bring you money. The only way to create something is to expend energy. Unfortunately there is no other way around it.

There are some dubious advisers and promoters around who will promise you incredibly high returns for little effort. Tempting though they might be, these schemes they are promoting also have to obey the laws of nature. You cannot get something for nothing, no matter how convincing the scheme may seem. Later in *Appreciating Assets,* we will look at some of these schemes. In the meantime, if it seems too good to be true, it is! Leave it alone, or you could find yourself on the wrong side of the bank or the Australian Tax Office. This is not a comfortable position to be in!

Fear of criticism from others. Zig Ziglar, one of America's top motivational speakers, coined the word 'SNIOP' in regards to a certain type of person. A Sniop is:

Susceptible to the Negative Influences of Other People.

They are less likely to invest in the first place and, when they do, can make disastrous decisions, based on the advice of others. They cannot act through self-confidence and are prone to believing that risk and loss will be the outcome of any decision they do make. They fear ridicule, criticism and making mistakes.

> ## "The majority of people who fail to accumulate money sufficient for their needs are generally easily influenced by the 'opinions of others'."
>
> Napoleon Hill

Charles Darwin had every reason to fear the criticism of some very powerful people, including the pope, archbishops and many scientists and philosophers. At the start of his life he was assessed as being mediocre in all areas of study. Of his school years he commented, "I believe that I was considered by all my masters, and by my father, as a very ordinary boy, rather below the common standards in intellect."

Ironically, at one point in his early life, he was destined to become a clergyman, but found he had little interest in such a profession. He eventually travelled on 'The Beagle' as a naturalist and, over five years, gathered enough information to begin his book, 'Origin of Species'. This book was followed, in 1871, by 'Descent of Man'.

Neither book pleased theologians or clerics very much. In fact, Darwin was mocked and reviled by some of the highest authorities in the Protestant and Catholic churches across the world. The contents of his work challenged the first book of the Old Testament. Darwin's evidence that species could change and evolve, that mankind itself was not made in the image of God and that we are closely related to primates did not win him any popularity contests, but he persevered in the face of controversy. He ignored the critics and, in doing so, he lost many friends. Today his theories and ideas are respected and accepted across the world, taught in schools and universities and even accepted by leading church authorities.

Many of us are perhaps a little more daunted than others by criticism and by other people's opinions of us. We all want to be accepted by others and fit in with a group. When a family member or close friend pours cold water on your plans and goals, it is hard to maintain faith in your ideas. If you are being told by half a dozen cautious and well-meaning friends or relatives that you are going to lose your money if you buy assets in whatever area or fund you have chosen, it is very easy to procrastinate or lose persistence.

Choose who you discuss your finances with carefully. As I have mentioned before, there will be much free advice offered from many who are less than adequately qualified or experienced to give such advice. If you are receiving criticism from someone whose only investment is a 'phone account at the TAB or a Lotto ticket every Monday, think about where their own advice has got them! Wherever possible, associate with people who are already wealthy or who are involved in asset accumulation and investment. The feedback from someone who has already done what you are about to do is invaluable. I recommend that my new clients talk to my existing clients and I even provide contact lists for that purpose. You cannot be an eagle if you fly with the crows.

Sometimes the accusation of selfishness or of 'risking' the family's financial stability is also thrown at you by 'well-meaning' family, friends and colleagues. The issue can become very emotional. Beware of thinking with your feelings at these times. Feelings and thoughts can easily be confused and this confusion can lead to some very expensive mistakes. Maintain calm and clarity and think with your head, not your heart.

If you have involved your immediate family in the initial decision and in the planning and setting of goals for creating wealth, and if they are clear on what will be gained and what the process will involve, it is likely that they will remain your allies in the face of criticism. (Criticism from parents, in-laws, siblings, friends, colleagues and anyone else who believes they can live your life more successfully than you can.)

If the family understands what is in it for the family as a whole and if their concerns and desires are listened to, acknowledged and accommodated wherever possible, their co-operation and support will be an asset and a positive influence.

If your children are old enough, it might be an excellent time to start educating them in these areas of financial management. It is unlikely that they are going to be taught to think with financial intelligence at school. I doubt they will learn it from their peers.

If they are concerned that changing the way you spend money will hamper their social acceptability, now might be a good time to suggest to them that neither mum nor dad is a cash-dispensing machine and explain the values to be gained from earning their own income. Throw in this quote from Napoleon Hill.

> "Anything acquired without effort and without cost is generally unappreciated, often discredited."

The quote may not be appreciated, but it might make you feel better! A set of earplugs can work wonders too!

How we can change our behaviours to create positive financial actions

How do we change attitudes that have been held for a lifetime or more? The attitudes towards money and wealth that your parents hold probably came from their parents and to some extent have probably been passed on to you.

As the bumper sticker says, "Attitudes are contagious. Make sure yours is worth catching!"

In this chapter we have looked at some of the attitudes and habits that have held us back from realising our financial goals. They are common habits. They are also dangerous habits. Becoming aware of them is the first step on the path to wealth. Getting rid of them and replacing them with good habits is the next step. In the following chapter we will look at a simple, effective plan that will, if followed with commitment, ambition, persistence and self-discipline, lead you to your financial goals.

HOW TO REALISE YOUR FINANCIAL GOALS

"I noticed that my poor dad was poor not because
of the amount of money he earned, which was
significant, but because of his thoughts and actions."
Robert T. Kiyosaki

Our minds are the origin of all perception and all action. How we choose to look at something affects what we see. Imagine three young children, all 12 years old, sitting on the kerb of a street in a large city. A cat strolls nonchalantly across the road towards them. Out of nowhere comes a car, travelling too fast to stop or swerve to miss the poor cat. The cat is flattened.

One child begins to scream and runs away to find Mum.

The second child bursts out laughing. "Did you see that! Did you see that!" he crows.

The third child stands up and looks at what is left of the cat. "Wow! Look at this, you can see the intestines. That's amazing. I never realised how long they are!"

Three very different reactions to the same event. Three very different ways of seeing the event. Admittedly, a somewhat gruesome way to illustrate that who we are and what we have learned as we grow affects what we perceive and how we react to an event.

In the same way we can follow how four different families will perceive, act and react to the same stimuli, the same information and the same events in the same economic climate.

Meet the families

Let me introduce you to four different families: the Brownlows, the Millers, the Turners and the Carringtons. While these families cannot represent every family structure in our culturally and socially diverse communities, they do represent the most common sets of attitudes, beliefs and habits regarding financial matters. In other words they represent the various levels of financial intelligence (or lack of it) we meet every day. They are based on the real stories of the thousands of people I have encountered through my work.

For convenience, we are assuming an average annual growth rate of 6 per cent for all families' investments and an average annual inflation rate of 4 per cent.

The Brownlows

The Brownlows subscribe to the "She'll be right! The government's been taking our tax, it owes us a pension" school of financial planning!

Richard and Ellen Brownlow live from week to week, just managing to get by on their joint incomes of $72,000 per annum. Richard is 50. He works full time for an engineering company and has been there for 15 years. Ellen is 49. She has a part time job as a receptionist at the local medical centre. Their two children are both at the local high school. Richard intends to retire in 15 years time, Ellen too. They owe $100,000 on their family home, which is currently worth $450,000. By the time they retire they will have superannuation savings of $300,000 and their home will be worth around $1,143,000.

Richard and Ellen cannot seem to save any money. They have no investment assets, but they do have recent-model cars, a small boat and trailer, a new kitchen and they have just bought their eldest son his first car. They manage to go on holiday twice a year. Richard believes that living comfortably and being able to afford life's little luxuries are more important than putting money away. He hasn't given a lot of thought to retirement, but isn't too worried. After all, they will both be eligible for a pension and they've got their super fund too! Besides, the way house prices have risen, their house will be worth over a million by the time they get to retirement. Once the kids have left home, they'll have more money and can put a bit more into the super fund. Richard reckons they'll be fine and Ellen takes her lead from him.

So let's look at what will have happened by the time they want to retire, in 15 years. Firstly they'll find that the pension they assumed was theirs either doesn't exist or is means-tested to the point where they are not eligible for more than a few dollars a week. Still they've got their super money. They could take that as a payout of a lump sum, minus taxes, or convert it to an income of around $18,000 a year. What will $18,000 buy in 16 years? It would buy just over half of what it buys today at an average 4 per cent annual inflation rate. This is not a future I would feel happy about. Through cynicism, ignorance and laziness the Brownlows are creating a future for themselves that very few people would like to live in. Their 'do nothing, it'll be all right' attitude will ensure their poverty and dependence at retirement.

The current cashflow of the Brownlow family

The crucial decisions that have shaped Richard and Ellen's story are, in chronological order:

Using money to buy liabilities. The Brownlows have been using their income to create liabilities, not assets. The boat, the extra car, the holidays and other extras that they have been putting their money into are not going to generate any returns for them in the future. The holidays leave memories and a few photographs, but that is all. The extra car is a

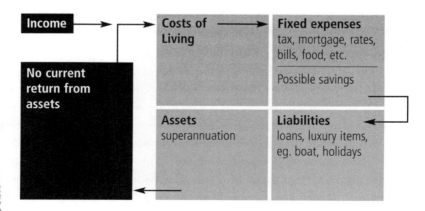

luxury that also sets a bad example to their eldest son, who has missed an opportunity to learn about saving for himself and realising a goal through his own hard work, not simply being handed it on a plate by his parents. The boat gives them a few hours of pleasure, but they might have been better off hiring one, since they use it infrequently and it spends most of its time on its trailer under wraps.

The other part of collecting liabilities is that they often create extra drain on income. The boat and car will need constant insurance and maintenance as well as running costs. They will age and depreciate, so will need replacement at some point. Most liabilities create extra costs.

Assuming the future will take care of itself.

This is a common decision, created by apathy, laziness, fear and pro-crastination. The future is our responsibility. Richard and Ellen are bury-ing their heads in the sand when it comes to their future. They have cho-sen to follow the creed that the government will look after them and so, why worry? This deliberate short-sightedness may remove the temporary discomfort of taking a long hard look at their finances, but will erode any chance they might have of creating a future they can look forward to.

Ignoring opportunities.

The Brownlows have opportunities at their fingertips, if they could only find the intent and the energy to follow them up. They earn, between them, $72,000 a year. The house they are living in is worth $450,000. They still owe $100,000 but the rest of it is theirs. This means they have $350,000 in equity that they could borrow against to invest, if they chose to do so. On earnings of nearly $1,400 a week, if they cur-tailed their heavy spending they could pay off their debts in three or four years and then begin to save hundreds a week, if they chose to do this. They are choosing to do nothing at the moment.

Refusing to look at the big picture.

Richard and Ellen are choosing to focus on the fantasy of being looked after by a government that will probably be unable to furnish an adequate pension for the millions of people who will be beyond retire-ment age when they themselves retire. If there is a gradual reduction in the proportion of people in the workforce paying taxes compared to those who have retired, you don't need to be Einstein to work out that the government is going to find it harder to fund aged care and welfare programs. If governments around the developed world are all aware of this fact and are all encouraging self-funded retirees through tax incentive schemes and rising superannuation contributions, surely it would make sense to read the writing on the wall and begin to do something about it now, whilst the opportunity is there?

A little assumption is a dangerous thing

The Brownlows have faith in the system. They've been paying their taxes. They'll be fine. They are assuming they'll get a pension and some super and it'll be all right. After all, their house will be worth over a million when they retire. True, but it will only give them a return if they sell it. Where will they live then? How much will it cost them to buy even a small house when they retire? What inflation and capital growth is doing to their house's value is also happening to every other house too. They have not thought it through. They refer to the future with assumptions and generalisations. This will cost them and their family dearly later on. At the very least it will mean they will have to sell the family home and move to a much smaller and cheaper one, probably in the cheaper suburbs and then exist on the returns from limited assets and a tiny pension. Not my idea of a pleasant future.

Jack and Sue

I will illustrate this further with the story of Jack and Sue. I met them a few years ago at one of my seminars. Jack had missed most of the seminar, he was working, but Sue sat through it all. Newly married, they had both been married before. Jack made child support payments for his children from the former marriage. He ran a consultancy and Sue worked with him. They made about $110,000 a year. Jack was 47 and wanted to retire at 55. He had $35,000 in his super fund. Sue had nothing. Their accountant suggested they put $40,000 a year into the super fund, even though they then found it hard to pay off the remaining loan of $47,000 on their house.

I pointed out to Jack that, even with the extra payments to his super fund each year, on retirement he would have about $400,000 in super. At 6 per cent return, he would get about $24,000 yearly income. With about $26,000 still owing on their home loan this would reduce their annual income to $22,000 from super. With an annual inflation rate of about 4 per cent, this would actually buy about three quarters of what it buys today by the time Jack retires. Jack reckoned that, because his accountant drove a Porsche, he must know what he was doing!

Sue was anxious to secure a better financial future and was excited by the investment returns that property could bring them. Her ex-husband had invested in long-term property investment and it was working beautifully for him. She knew Jack's super was not going to be enough for a comfortable, independent retirement. She wanted to schedule another meeting with me so I asked her to get Jack to go through some questions with him before we made a time to meet.

The questions:

- Will you have enough assets to be financially independent on retirement?
- Do you believe the government will look after you in retirement?
- Is there anyone else who will look after you when you retire?
- Do you think money in the bank is a good investment?
- Do you think you can pick the right shares and can you afford to buy enough?
- Do you know anyone who has lost money on prime-position property in Sydney that they have held for 10 years or more?

Jack remained cynical at first, but I am scheduled to meet with them as I write this, so hopefully we can work on a plan they are both happy with, beginning with the end in mind. Jack's accountant has created a plan to have them retire on less than $500 a week. They can do much, much better! Hopefully Sue can persuade Jack that his accountant, whilst a wonderful accountant, is not the best person to give them financial investment advice. Even if he does drive a Porsche!

Ian and Helen

Another family's story shows us how fear and cynicism will erode chances of a financially secure and comfortable future. Ian and his wife, Helen, came to another of my seminars and seemed excited by what I had to say. They made an appointment to see me. We went through the existing figures. They lived in West Pennant Hills in Sydney with their two children. Ian had about $40,000 in super and wanted to retire at 60. Projecting this figure forward at 6 per cent annual growth, Ian would have $340,000 in super and would have paid off their family home two years before retirement. This would have given him a retirement income of $18,000. Not enough, they agreed.

So we looked at their budget and found a way to pay off the house eight years earlier. We looked at his tax situation and worked out that they could afford to buy a one-bedroom apartment in Pyrmont in the inner city of Sydney, so giving them rental income, tax rebates and investment growth well over the average 6 per cent figure. Their bank looked at the figures and agreed. Their solicitor looked at the contract and gave it his approval. They were all set to borrow, to invest and to secure an independent financial future. Then Ian read in the paper that we may be heading for a recession. He pulled out!

Needless to say, we haven't yet reached that recession and the investor that did buy Ian's property has watched it increase in value from the day he bought it. The moral of this story is, if you believe everything you read in the paper, you may find life a very scary place! Remember, bad news sells papers. Forecasts of doom and gloom happen in the media every day. Ian's fear and cynicism will cost him and his family dearly. There is no perfect time to buy, there is only NOW!

All the families above, the Brownlows, Jack and Sue, Ian and Helen will end up in the 95 per cent of people that retire on less than $25,000 a year. They didn't have to, they chose to. Fear, ignorance, cynicism, procrastination, laziness and being influenced by negative opinions of others have influenced their choices.

The Millers

The Millers subscribe to the "We've been brought up to believe that debt is a bad, bad thing and to be avoided wherever possible" school of financial planning!

Steven and Michelle Miller live in Thornleigh in the north-west of Sydney. Both are in their mid-forties and want to retire in 16 years. Their children still live with them. One is at university and the other is in the final year at high school. Steven has worked out his super fund will be worth about $300,000, or $18,000 as a yearly income on retirement. Not enough. Steven and Michelle have decided to buy an investment property but are scared of borrowing more than they have to and are scared of using their family home as equity, just in case. So they have spent the last three years struggling to save a 10 per cent deposit for the property. They managed to save $15,000 and purchased a three-bedroom brick and tile unit, 14 years old, for $120,000, in the western suburbs of Sydney. They had to buy there because it was all they could afford without using the equity on their own home.

The unit is miles away from anywhere, in an average state of repair and in a low capital growth area (compared with the property capital growth around the inner cities – see chapter 6). Since they've bought it nine months ago they've had five weeks vacancy and they have just had to evict the last tenant for non-payment of rent and damage to carpets, blinds and paintwork. They estimate it will be worth about $224,000 by the time they want to retire. They will have been able to pay it off by then, as long as they watch every cent they spend from now until then. Then they can sell it, leaving a profit of $178,000 after sales costs and capital gains tax, which can then be put in managed funds at 6 per cent giving them around $11,000 extra a year. Or they can continue to rent it out for about $9,000 a year. So, when they retire, they will have made it into the elite 5 per cent who retire on more than $25,000 a year – just!

With their super income and rent, or managed funds income they will be living on around $28,000 a year. Again, factoring in the effects of inflation after 16 years, it is obvious that they will have little to spend on anything but the bare necessities. They have saved and scrimped for years to buy and maintain this investment property, but it is still not enough.

The current cashflow of the Miller family

The decisions that have shaped the Millers' future are:

Considering the big picture.

The Millers started off well by looking at their future and realising that working hard for forty years is not enough to guarantee a prosperous and comfortable retirement. They have the right intentions, but have chosen an ineffective way of aiming for their future financial independence.

Allowing fear to interfere with a plan of action.

They have a fear of getting into debt, which is common with many people, and have allowed that fear to choose the path they will travel on

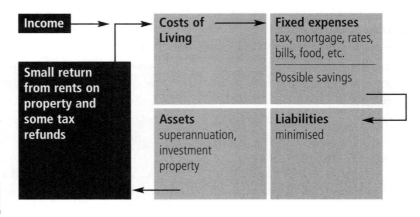

to reach their goal. They have limited their options, through this fear, and have limited their returns because of this. Not all debt is bad debt. The returns from an investment such as prime real estate are much higher than the property they have chosen. They believed they could not afford to buy prime and so went for inferior property.

Not seeking advice from the experts.

If they had been fully informed of their options and had been shown different ways to approach property investment, they would have been better off in the long run. An expert could have explained the difference between good, constructive debt and bad, destructive debt. If they had borrowed enough to secure a piece of prime real estate, like the Turners and Carringtons, all their hard work and planning would have give them their just deserts, as opposed to the very poor results that they will see in their future.

Ineffective planning.

Without the right advice, their planning lacks several elements. They have no idea how much they will need to live on in retirement. They have no real idea of how much their existing investment will give them in the future. They have not planned to use the returns or equity from their investment to set up subsequent investments, so generating better returns in the future. They have not researched the rental market and so have no idea what they are letting themselves in for. They have not fac-tored in the consequences of buying a cheap property in the middle of nowhere in terms of attracting the right tenant or of the cost of main-taining such a property.

They looked at the big picture, but only focused on a very small part of it. This will mean that their retirement will be a struggle to make ends meet and to afford any of the luxuries of life, such as holidays, entertain-ment, eating out or the other non-essentials that make the difference between surviving and living.

Damien

Damien, currently an investor through REIN, had, for many years, laboured under the illusion that the less money you borrowed in regards to property investment, the quicker you could recoup a profit from the investment. In 1990 he decided to invest in a local property, a unit 10 minutes north of the Wollongong CBD in NSW. The unit was 20 years old with two bedrooms, in good condition and only cost $69,000. He made a few renovations, put in a new carpet and gave it a fresh coat of paint before letting it out at $110 a week. After the first tenants left, he found it hard to secure another tenant, so dropped the rent to $105 a week. This tenant, and the subsequent one, fell behind in their rents and caused much damage to the unit. Third time lucky, or so he thought. He got a good tenant, but, after a year, she left, due to harassment and threats from the less than lovable tenants in the unit next door.

The place remained untenanted for five months, so he sacked the estate agent and found his own tenant. This tenant lost her job and stopped paying rent. Three court hearings and one eviction later, he was back to an empty property and no rent. He decided to sell the unit and placed it on the market in 1998. Now married with a child, he had had enough. There were no takers, so he kept trying to tenant it whilst waiting for the market to pick up. He kept on losing money through tenants not paying and jumping ship. Early in 2000 it was back on the market and eventually was sold in mid 2000 for, you guessed it, $69,000, the same price he paid for it 10 years before!

I'll let him sum up in his own words.

"I have now made considerably more money in the space of three weeks buying a property through REIN than I did in 10 years with a property near Wollongong. I keep reminding myself of the old saying, LOCATION, LOCATION, LOCATION! Never again!"

In a nutshell, he had the right intentions, but he made an unwise choice of investment. He bought what he thought was all he could afford at the time. When he began, he did not have the concept of borrowing using equity in existing assets, such as the family home, to increase the rate of earnings on a well-researched and well-chosen investment property. It took 10 years of banging his head against sporadically-tenanted and damaged brick walls to put him on the right track.

If it's any consolation to Damien, he isn't alone. There are thousands of horror stories told along these lines, where people buy the wrong property, which can only attract the wrong tenant, or no tenant at all. In fact, it is these stories that have created such bad press for investment properties, giving rise to the fears of tenants from hell, no tenants at all and slow capital growth. However these fears need not be realised if you are willing to take some simple steps that will give you a start on the road to successful investment for a comfortable future and a life lived, rather than survived.

Simone and Peter

Take the example offered by Simone and Pete, another couple I met through a seminar. By the time they were 42 they had paid off their family home and were raising three children. Financially, they decided to invest in property. They had saved $5,000, which went as deposit on a $92,000 free-standing home in Sydney's south-west. It was 20 years old and only needed a little work to make it a viable rental property. They did their sums. They were paying off the loan as an interest-only loan at 7.2 per cent for five years. Their weekly interest bill was $121. The rent was $90 a week, which left them to find the extra $31 a week.

They felt so confident that they went back to the bank and used the equity on their own home to finance the purchase of two more properties for $110,000 and $112,000. Both were free-standing houses, 15 and 20 years old, both in Sydney's south-west. They had borrowed another $240,000 to cover purchases and costs. The houses were tenanted at $95 and $100 a week. The cost to them of the interest-only loans on these two houses was $332 a week. They needed to find an extra $137 a week to cover the new properties.

So they were now paying $168 a week to hold these properties. The other costs, rates, agent's commission, insurance and maintenance added another $130 a week. So, for the privilege of owning three older suburban rental properties, they were paying $297 a week.

Some investment! They had not done their homework. The areas they bought into had had less than 2 per cent average yearly capital growth in the previous five years. The properties were old, had higher maintenance costs than newer properties and they had trouble finding and keeping the right kind of tenant.

ARTCHA '02

Like so many other people, they did not seek professional advice, they did not do the research and they risked their financial futures. All the above are commended for their good intentions, but they illustrate the point that, to make blind or uninformed decisions can be worse than doing nothing at all. So what can you do to improve on these performances? Perhaps the Turners can demonstrate.

The Turner family

The Turners subscribe to the "We've done our homework, we know what we want, we know what we have to do to get it!" school of financial planning!

The Turners start off from the same position as the Brownlows and Millers. They have two children, both at high school. Their own family home is worth $450,000 and they owe $100,000 on it. They will receive about $300,000 as a super payout on retirement in 16 years, which they will rollover to generate $18,000 a year income, the same as the previous two families. The difference is that they decided to seek advice from both professionals and from those who have already invested successfully in residential property.

The next step for the Turners was to start a process of debt reduction through budgeting. This does not mean they live on bread and water for the next sixteen years. It means they set realistic goals and put any extra income into reducing the debt still owing on their house, whilst using the existing equity to purchase premium property in an area showing high capital growth (at least doubling in value over 10-12 years, a capital growth of around 6 per cent per annum) and higher-than-average rent returns. It also means they will pay their own house off earlier and so have more money to put into further investment, if they so choose.

They were advised to buy a property with the tenant in mind. They were looking to buy a tenant first! They chose the CBD and then chose the apartment that would secure the type of tenant that could afford to pay the rent they wanted. The tenant, as we see in more detail later in the book, is not paying for accommodation, but is paying for a lifestyle. This lifestyle includes a view, high levels of comfort, all mod cons, security, pool, sauna and gym at their doorstep. There is no need for commuting or a car and easy access to public transport, restaurants, cafes, cinemas and shops, all less than five minutes walk away. Absolute convenience.

The Turners bought a one-bedroom apartment in a new development in Sydney's CBD for $380,000. They took out a total loan of

$400,000. The apartment was bought 'off the plan'. It hadn't even been built at this point! By the time they came to settlement day, the property was already valued at $430,000.

That's $50,000 increase in value in less than a year!

The Turners bought without a deposit, using the equity in their own home. They got the right advice, which meant that, with an interest-only loan, with full tax rebates and tax efficiency, their holding costs to start with were only $40 to $50 a week. The property in the north end of the CBD's 'dress circle' offered excellent capital growth. By the time they want to retire, the property will be worth at least $1,000,000.

If they choose to sell at this point, they will need to pay out the original $400,000 loan, about $162,000 in capital gains tax (subject to rules at the time) and about $27,000 in sales costs. This leaves them with a profit of $411,000. If they invest this in managed funds at a conservative 6 per cent per annum, they will have a yearly income of $25,000 from the managed funds and a further $18,000 a year from their super fund so giving them an income of $43,000 a year.

How did they manage to do this?

The current cashflow of the Turner family

The decisions the Turners made to reach their goal were:

Seeing the big picture.

The Turners have not only looked at the big picture, they have looked at all of it carefully. They are aware of their choices and have made

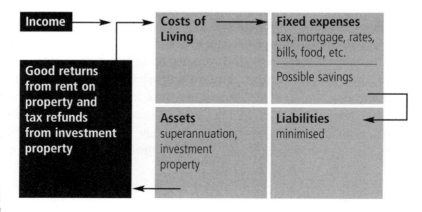

them with the big picture held firmly in mind. They do not expect to rely on anyone but themselves for their future and have taken responsibility for creating that future.

Getting the right advice.

Their first step was to get advice from the experts. They spoke to professional investment advisers and also to friends and acquaintances who were already investing successfully. They did their homework and selected property as their chosen vehicle of investment. They then spoke to property investment specialists and even contacted existing clients of the service that interested them the most.

Creating an effective plan.

The next step was to create an effective plan. They worked out how much they would need to retire comfortably and then, working backwards from this figure, worked out the level of investment they needed.

Reducing existing debts and implementing a savings plan.

They looked at their expenditure and their income and decided to create a budget which would get rid of existing debts quicker, such as the $100,000 owing on their family home and the money owed on their credit cards. Once these were paid off, the money would be diverted to generating better returns from existing investments or generating more assets. They involved the whole of their family, so the children would understand and be more supportive. They even got the children to help design the budget! By increasing the money they were paying off on their mortgage and reducing themselves to one credit card account, paid off monthly, they reduced their interest payments and were able to pay off their home much more quickly.

Recognising opportunity.

They bought their prime real estate 'off the plan', before it had been built. This saved them tens of thousands of dollars on the price. They chose the unit to attract a certain type of tenant, so their research and planning would pay off and they would not have to worry too much about vacancies and damage. They had worked out their finances and felt confident of affording their investment. They used the tax benefits, put in place by the government to encourage the purchase of investment property, to pay for most of the costs!

Acting immediately on their plan.

They began immediately. They started the research as soon as they had decided to invest. They started the budget as soon as they knew what they were going to invest in and how they would do it. They bought off the plan, from the design stage of the development, which meant that they saved tens of thousands and secured a prime real estate asset.

Using leverage to generate returns.

There is a key concept here that applies to all investments. Leverage. The Turners used it to enable them to generate the returns they needed for successful retirement. It needs to be considered in some detail, because of its importance in wealth creation.

Leverage and investment growth

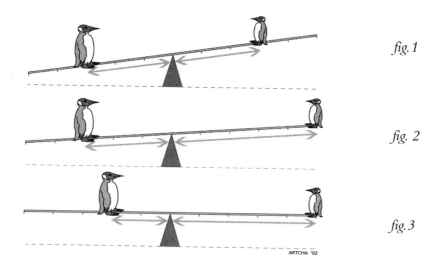

fig. 1

fig. 2

fig.3

ARTCHA '02

Imagine two objects balancing on a seesaw. One object is 20kg heavier than the other. If the objects are placed the same distance away from the middle of the seesaw (the fulcrum, or balancing point) the heavier object will go down and the lighter object will go up (fig. 1). If the lighter object moves down, away from the balancing point, increasing the distance from the centre of the seesaw, its weight doesn't change but the effects of it are increased by the distance (fig. 2). There will be a point on this seesaw where the lighter object can sit and balance the heavier object. The same applies if the heavier object moves in towards the middle, decreasing the distance (fig. 3). The effects of that object's weight decreases. This can be seen to work with investments when you calculate compound interest on two different amounts. Let's imagine that Mrs Jones, at 40, has invested $20,000 at an average return of 6 per cent, to be used for income when she is 60. She has the interest automatically reinvested into her fund. Over 20 years she will earn interest, and then interest on the interest, and then interest on the interest on the interest and so on. By the time she is 60, her fund will be worth over $64,000. If she invests double the amount ($40,000) she will get over $128,000 in 20 years, all without adding another cent from her own pocket.

Now back to the seesaw. If we swap 'weight' for 'amount of money' and 'distance' for 'time', as you increase the amount of money or the time, the effects on the invested amount multiply. Whether it is compound interest or capital growth of an asset, the more you put in and the longer you leave it, the greater the value of your asset.

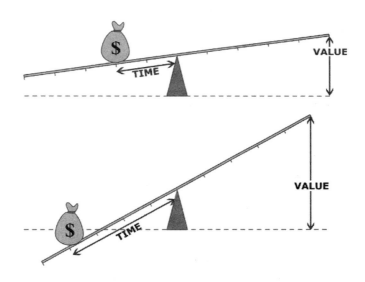

Now imagine Mrs Jones has decided to invest. The capital growth of her investment will rise over the years, regardless of whatever vehicle she has decided to invest in, shares, property or managed funds. She has decided on a property. She has only 20 years to make this investment pay for her retirement. Obviously, the more she can invest at Year 1, the more she will be able to make by Year 20. She can just afford a deposit of 10 per cent on an investment property of $150,000. She buys a two-bedroom unit out in the western suburbs of her home city. By the time she retires it will, in theory, be worth around $300,000. (I say 'in theory'

because capital growth of properties out in the suburbs is slower than that in the inner city or more desirable locations. If 6 per cent is the average capital growth, then some properties will grow at less than this average figure, and some will grow more than the average figure. My money is on such a property as giving less than average capital growth.)

So, returning to Mrs Jones's financial situation. She borrowed $140,000 to buy the unit and cover her costs. She took out an interest-only loan and the rent and her tax rebates covered the interest costs over the 20 years. When she sold the place she paid back the $140,000, the capital gains tax and the sales costs (around $61,000), which left her with $100,000 profit. What if she had borrowed more money in the first place, thus increasing the effectiveness of her investment through leverage?

Imagine she decides to borrow $300,000, using the equity of her family home.

She still takes it out as an interest-only loan. She will be able to buy a unit that will command a higher rent. This will also, with the increase in tax rebates, enable her to cover the interest costs of the unit over 20 years. In 20 years time the unit will be worth around $600,000. She sells, pays off the loan ($300,000) the capital gains tax and sales costs, around $120,000 and is left with $180,000 profit. Through increasing the amount she borrowed, through increasing the effect of leverage, she has increased the money she has to retire on by $80,000. At 6 per cent returns in managed funds, she has increased her yearly retirement income by $5,000! And it has cost her no extra. All she needed was the financial intelligence and courage to use debt constructively and make leverage work for her investment.

Add a little more courage. Let's say she borrows $420,000 to buy an investment unit. 20 years down the track it will be worth $900,000. She sells, pays out the loan, the tax and costs of about $170,000 and is left with $310,000 profit. This is three times the profit she would have made if she had bought the original two-bedroom unit out in the west. An extra $12,000 a year retirement income, just through increasing her lever-age. And, again, at no extra cost to her. Yes, her interest payments go up, but so do the rent and the amount of tax rebates available. Over 20 years, with increases in rent and the effects of inflation, the unit will have cov-ered its own costs.

Simply because Mrs Jones has the courage and the intelligence to make other people's money work for her with minimal risk and minimal outlay from her, she will be able to secure a comfortable retirement

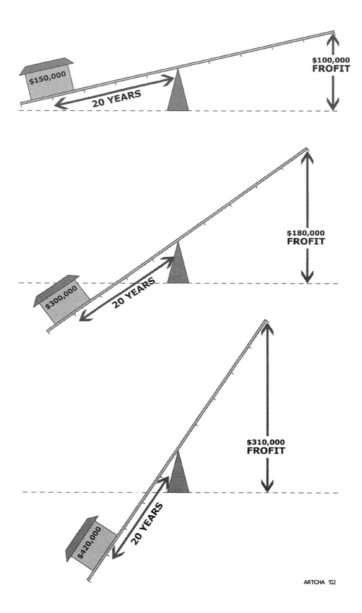

ARTCHA '02

income! This is how the rich get rich and stay rich. They use other people's money to increase the effects of leverage!

Following this through logically, why stop at one? Why not double or triple your leverage and invest in several properties? It's time to meet the Carringtons!

The Carringtons

This family subscribes to the "Show me the money!" school of financial planning!

The Carringtons are just like the other three families in their physical make-up. Two children at high school, paying off a family home, currently worth $450,000 on which they owe $100,000. Luke and Helga Carrington will have around $300,000 in super when they retire in 16 years. This is where the similarity ends. Luke is an ambitious man who has always prided himself on his ability to see the big picture and to calculate and manage risks. He has a dream! A dream of 30 years spent sailing, playing golf and gardening. Helga wants to learn painting and drawing and wants to travel around Africa and South America.

They have a plan to achieve their dream and they have access to good advisers and the information and skills needed to put this plan into action. They have worked hard for everything they have and understand that sheer hard work alone cannot give them a wealthy lifestyle. How many of you are still struggling financially, in spite of all your sheer hard work? Financial intelligence and strong motivation are needed. They want to be able to retire wealthy. They have calculated how much they would need to be wealthy and have come up with a figure of $100,000 a year.

This year they are going to use the equity in their own home to invest in a $400,000 apartment in Sydney's CBD. They will need to borrow $420,000 through an interest-only loan, which will cover all costs. They calculate that they will have paid off their family home within the next two years. This will enable them to take out a second interest-only loan on another investment property in two years. Their first investment property will have increased in value already, whilst the amount of principal owed to the bank stays constant. They are keen on buying 'off the plan' (see chapter 8 for more information on this) and so they are estimating that, even in only two years, the value of property one (**P1**) will have risen by around $80,000.

Just in time for property two (**P2**). They will buy the next property for $480,000, using the equity in the family home and **P1**. They will actually take out a loan of $520,000 to cover all costs. Two more years and a further increase in value of the family home, **P1** and **P2** (also bought 'off the plan') means they can buy property three (**P3**) at $560,000, with a loan of $590,000 to cover all costs. Again they want to buy 'off the plan' so, by the time they want to buy property four (**P4**), four years after **P3,** they will have enough increase in value of all their property holdings to generate enough equity for the $670,000 interest-only loan to buy **P4** for $640,000. Six years after the purchase of **P4** they want to retire. Where will they be financially?

They will have total loans owing to the bank of $2,200,000! They will have four investment properties worth around $4,000,000 in total. They will sell them all off and, once they have paid out the capital gains tax and selling costs, as well as the amount owed to the bank, they will have a profit of around $1,500,000! If they invest this at 6 per cent in managed funds, this will generate around $90,000 a year. Add the $18,000 from their super funds and they will be receiving a gross amount of $108,000 a year in retirement.

The Carringtons have put aside fear and cynicism to generate wealth. They have used leverage and have used over $2 million of some-body else's money to create a future worth looking forward to! It is a huge amount of debt though, so the Carringtons have insured themselves through income protection, death cover and rental insurance cover. Remember the old saying, "It's no good spoiling the ship for a ha'porth of tar". I doubt the Carringtons would risk such a large debt without these insurances, which would work out to be less than half a percent of the total profit on these properties. They are financially intelligent people, not reckless gamblers! They got good advice and had the courage and intelligence to follow through.

The cashflow of the Carrington family

The crucial decisions made to enable the creation of wealth were:
Seeing the big picture.
The Carringtons, just like the Turners, took a long hard look at the big picture and kept it in the front of their minds. They worked out how they wanted to live in retirement and how much money they would need to do this. They worked out how much money they would need to invest and what returns they would need to generate. Then they worked out the most efficient way of investing, considering initial start-up costs and the time needed for their investments to generate the required level of return.

Getting the right advice.
They sought professional advice and also the advice of those who had already done what they wanted to do. They explained their goals and

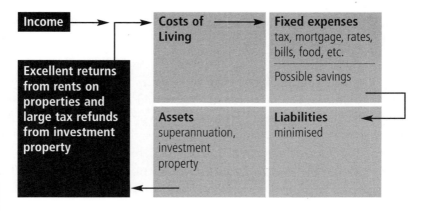

intentions clearly so that they would get appropriate information and contacts. They acted quickly and responsibly, able to recognise opportunities and safeguard their assets as much as possible, because they had the right advice.

Facing fear and cynicism.

They researched and checked and double-checked all their figures until they were confident they could be successful in their investment venture. They refused to be influenced by negative comments from negative people. They talked to people who were already doing what they were about to do. Their advice and feedback was more important and accurate than the mother-in-law's or the neighbour's opinions on how dangerous investment was or how house prices were going to slump to an all-time low in a matter of months. They refused to let the ignorant or inexperienced influence their decisions. They used intelligence and only borrowed what they knew could be paid back at a later stage, after it had increased their financial nest egg. They took out all the relevant insurances and double-checked everything they could. They entered into their investment plan with open eyes and informed minds.

Using one asset to help build another and another.

Starting with the asset of the equity in their own home the Carringtons began to build a new asset. This, in turn, increased their equity to the point where they could borrow enough to generate another asset, and so on. By using the equity in their previous assets they were able to borrow enough to make their investment plan work. They used an increasing leverage to build their assets up to level they had calculated was sufficient for them to live the way they wanted to, not the way they had to.

Persistence.

The Carringtons knew they were in for the long haul. They knew that any drop in the property market would be followed by a rise and knew that holding on and perseverance would pay in long run. Again, because they had a clear and effective plan, the right advice and an eye on the big picture, they were forewarned, forearmed and looking forward to the goal at the end of their investment plan. Their wealth will not be created by luck, but by hard work, informed decisions, educated assessments of risk and a focus on the rewards at the end.

Tom and Sarah

Tom and Sarah met me at a seminar in 1997. They were a fairly typical couple, two children, own home not yet paid off. Tom was 46. Their income was $85,000 a year before tax. After tax, they were getting $56,595. They worked out with me what they would need to retire and came up with $80,000 a year. Time was not on their side. Tom wanted to retire in 14 years and, in order to reach their desired retirement income, multiple property investment was the only option. They worked through a plan and decided to buy four properties over the next few years.

The first purchase in 1997 was in Chatswood on Sydney's north shore. They paid $220,000 for a one-bedroom unit. The second purchase in 1999 was in Pyrmont, on the edge of Sydney's CBD, for $245,000. The third was another Pyrmont property for $480,000. The fourth was in the following year, also on the edge of the CBD, for another $480,000. Tom and Sarah looked at their existing income and worked out a budget whereby they could pay off the family home within seven years and then pay out the first property's loan before Tom's 60th birthday.

Where will they be on Tom's 60th birthday? Their total debt to the bank would be $1,260,000. Their total property value on retirement will be around $2,551,000. Once they have paid out the loans, the capital gains tax and the selling costs of around $394,000, they will have $897,000 to invest for retirement. At 6 per cent this generates $53,820. Add to this the money from his super fund, which will be around $380,000 by then, at 6 per cent, which gives them another $22,000 and they are only $4,000 a year short of their goal of $80,000 a year.

56

Graham

Graham made a decision to invest several years ago out of a strong desire to increase and maintain his family's personal wealth. He and his wife were both working and had a good double income. They had paid off most of their own home. Graham came to a seminar I ran and stayed behind to chat to me. We then made an appointment to meet and go through financial projections. He was happy to be involved and commented on the simplicity of the whole process and the wealth of information and research I provided for him before he made a decision.

He decided to work on buying several properties and worked out how much risk he was willing to take through the Loan to Value ratio (LVR) calculated and monitored by the bank. In the initial stages this LVR was high, which meant the risk was high, but both Graham and the bank were happy with that level of risk. As the properties increased in value and as he began paying off equity, the LVR dropped quite quickly. (See chapter 7 – 'How to get hold of other people's money' for a detailed examination of LVR).

Graham bought 'off the plan' and when the buildings were completed, they were all worth tens of thousands of dollars more, on settlement, than Graham actually paid.

Graham and his family are currently living overseas and are looking forward to retirement with wealth and choice. Graham and his wife have realised their dreams of buying a beautiful house in Sydney and having a high standard of living that will allow them to travel where they want, when they want, in a few years time.

Philip and Amula

Philip and his wife, Amula, came to see me six years ago. They currently own four properties, with another four planned. They wanted to be wealthy on retirement and were willing to work hard for their ideal lifestyle. They started when they were in their late thirties and have worked out a goal income for their retirement of $120,000 a year, after tax! They want to live on $300 or more a day! As Philip put it, "You're a long time retired! Why not enjoy it?"

When they came to our first meeting, the qualities that stood out in them were drive and ambition, commitment, courage and independence. They convinced me that they were ready and able to develop and put into action an investment plan involving at least eight properties.

Firstly we needed to work out how large Philip's investments had to be to get his target income of $120,000 net each year. If the couple are each deemed to be earning $85,000 from their investments, then they will each end up with around $60,000 after tax, which adds up to their goal income. This means the investment must bring in $170,000 a year before tax. If we project that they will be getting a return on their investments of around 6 per cent a year, they need to invest around $2,800,000 at 6 per cent to get the income they want!

How will they do this?

- Their joint superannuation will be worth around $500,000 when they retire.
- They already own four properties and intend to buy four more. They used the equity in their own home to buy the first property and went from there, building up their equity and borrowing on that equity to buy subsequent properties.
- They used interest–only loans to buy the properties.
- They will only buy premium CBD apartments and they have been buying these 'off the plan' to save money. They are both working and bring in a joint income of $108,000 a year. They have worked out a budget and stick to it rigorously. (For a detailed explanation of this process, read chapters 6, 7 and 8.)
- When they reach their late 50s they will retire, sell the properties and invest the profits in a managed fund at around 6 per cent a year.

The following table shows what profits they stand to make if they use their plan to guide them.

Projected profits for Philip and Amula's property portfolio

Property number (P)	Year of purchase	Original loan value	Estimated value in 2020	Profit after loan repayment, sales costs and CGT
P1	1996	$ 220,000	$ 840,000	$ 460,000
P2	1997	$ 240,000	$ 900,000	$ 490,000
P3	1999	$ 290,000	$ 940,000	$ 470,000
P4	2001	$ 370,000	$ 1,050,000	$ 480,000
P5	2003	$ 420,000	$ 1,100,000	$ 470,000

P6	2005	$ 450,000	$ 1,060,000	$ 410,000
P7	2007	$ 470,000	$ 910,000	$ 270,000
P8	2009	$ 510,000	$ 920,000	$ 235,000

The total profit will be $3,285,000. If this is invested at 6 per cent it will give them around $190,000 a year gross income. The net worth will be around $130,000 a year. This has not included the money from their super funds. They are looking at a very comfortable lifestyle on retirement. Philip always wanted the ability to say, "Where shall we go today?" and then go there! If they follow their plan to the end they will be able to go anywhere at any time! This level of investment and borrowing is not for everyone, but Philip has worked it out carefully, has got the best advice possible – and has covered his family with every insurance he can. He likes to sleep at night too!

Over 40 per cent of the clients I work with buy more than one property as part of their financial plan. Through talking to them I make sure they are able to handle multiple property investments. I look for several key characteristics. They need to have a clear plan and be committed to long-term investment. They must be confident and strong in their beliefs. They need resilience to withstand the pressures and interference from well-meaning but ignorant friends and family. They need to be willing to follow the six steps outlined below to realise their financial goals.

Six steps to realising financial goals

One way of ensuring that you can begin the realisation of your financial goals is to follow six simple steps. If you follow these steps with commitment, persistence, strong desire and motivation, the frame of mind you are creating inside your head will lead you to the financial independence and stability that you desire.

"Preceding accomplishment
must be desire. The desires
must be strong and definite."

George S. Clason

Clason goes on to explain, "General desires are but weak longings. For a man to wish to be rich is of little purpose. For a man to desire five pieces of gold is a tangible desire which he can press to fulfillment. In learning to secure his one definite small desire, he hath trained himself to secure a larger one. This is the process by which wealth is accumulated." So, on this basis:

1) Fix in your mind the exact amount of money you want to enable you to achieve the lifestyle you want in retirement. In chapter 8, I will show you how to do this accurately and easily, by creating a detailed picture of your own 'compelling future'.

2) Determine exactly what you intend to give in return for the money. What is acceptable to you and your family? What luxuries and extravagances must fall by the wayside in your quest for a brighter future? If only one of you is currently working, assuming of course that you are a couple, could the other perhaps work also, to increase income for the next few years? If you run two new cars, upgrading them every three years, could you exist on one car or only upgrade one car and allow the other to age a little longer? It will take some effort and input on your part. What are you willing to do to make this future real? Again, in chapter 8 there is more detailed information on budgets and paying off loans.

3) Establish a definite date by which you will have achieved your goals. If necessary, break down the route into stages and date the completion of each stage. The stages could look like this:

Stage 1. Work out and implement budget by New Year's Eve.

Stage 2. Increase payments on existing mortgage by $150 a month by the end of January.

Stage 3. Organise with bank for interest-only equity loan in order to purchase investment property by the end of April.

Stage 4. Purchase investment property by the end of July.

Stage 5. Pay off first mortgage within five years and set up a new mortgage on the investment property, redirecting the original mortgage payments to the new mortgage.

Stage 6. Pay off first investment property before retirement on my 60th birthday.

4) Create a definite plan for carrying out each stage of your goal, and begin at once. Following the above example, you could begin with Stage 1 by calculating your current expenditures and incomes, in order to work out your new budget. However you have structured your goal plan, the important thing is to make a start. What is one thing you could do NOW to begin the journey to financial independence?

5) Write out a clear and concise statement of all the above steps. Here is a simple and clear statement, based on the plan above.

"We will need to be generating $45,000 a year through investments and superannuation by the time I reach my sixtieth birthday. We will achieve this by creating and maintaining a budget, increasing our mortgage repayments, buying an investment property, paying off our house within five years from now and paying off the investment property before I retire."

6) Read your written statement aloud, twice daily. Pin it up on a wall or stick it on the mirror. Have it in front of you. As you read it, imagine yourself in retirement, living the lifestyle you are aiming for. What will it look like? What will it feel like? What will you be doing? How will you be living? It is vital to keep this mental image of living your goal as if you have already achieved it.

Successful sportsmen and women know the secret to winning is to visualise the outcome of winning in their minds before they begin. By running a program for success through the brain before they engage in their chosen sport, they increase their chances of winning dramatically. This mental imagery is actually a part of the training devised by the Australian Institute of Sport to create elite sportsmen and women. If it works for them, it will work for you. How many medals do you think Ian Thorpe would have won if he had entertained images of drowning whilst waiting poolside for his events to start? Probably none!

What successful people share is a definite purpose, fuelled by a strong desire for its achievement. Successful people have a definite plan, which they act upon immediately and with persistence and effort. They close their minds against the negativity and discouragement of people who tell them they cannot do it. They open their minds and ears to the people who have already done it and can help and encourage them to follow through with their plans and their purpose.

Making your money work harder

Most people have spent their lives stretching their expenditure to meet their income, whatever it is. Many of you know only too well the struggle to make it through to the start of the next pay period, even after you have just been given a rise in income. Some of you will also have been lucky enough to win or inherit money only to have had it trickle through your fingers. This common trait is shared by many and is derived from the lack of clear goals and a plan to make them reality. Once you have this plan to reach your goal in place and have created the picture of having reached your goal in your mind, you will find that any money that does come into your hands has the last drop of value squeezed from it before you let it go.

> ## "I found the road to wealth when I decided that a part of all I earned was mine to keep."
>
> George S. Clason

One habit that evades many people is the habit of paying themselves first. This habit alone will kickstart your generation of income. Imagine you have just received your weekly pay as cash in your hand. What will you do with it? Pay bills, pay the mortgage and any other loan, buy food and petrol and with the little that is left, buy a few extras. Now your hand is empty and you have nothing to show for it. Nothing you have paid out for is earning you anything.

Consider this scenario. You have the same amount of money in your hand. First, before anything else, you remove 10 per cent of the total amount. Now you pay bills, mortgage and other loan instalments, buy petrol and spend the rest on food and other necessary groceries. You still have the 10 per cent and you probably didn't even miss it.

Now use that money where it can most help you achieve your goal, according to your plan, and maintain that habit. Some people even find they can divert more than 10 per cent. The more, the better. What you are doing is breaking the habit of living up to your income.

Another way of paying yourself first works well too. Every day that you get home from work, the shops, wherever you have been, have a large moneybox, bowl or jar near the front door. As you pass it, empty your pockets or purse and place all your coins in it. Once it is full, take it to the bank and make extra payments on your mortgage. By doing that, you will reduce the amount of interest you have to pay the bank. If you do it on a regular basis you will save thousands in interest repayments and own your own home sooner. All from a handful of change a day!

Little x often = a lot

A friend of mine, Sylvie, found herself starting from scratch after a recent divorce. As a sole parent with a very low income (less than $20,000 a year) she still knew she had to do something immediately to build some sort of financial future. She diverted all of her silver coins into a moneybox for her son. In spite of her low income she found she did not miss the silver. Her son is just five years old and now has a managed fund with over $2,000 in it! She has been diverting all gold coins to her own money box for a few months now and has been able set up a fund for herself.

She continues to add to both funds by diverting coins. She has now begun to divert 10 per cent of her income to her own fund. When she receives any income increase or extra earnings she diverts this bonus straight to the funds. She maintains a strict budget and pays herself and her son before she pays anyone else. This woman is on the lowest income of all my acquaintances, yet is still able to begin creating a better financial future for both her and her son.

Sudden gains

Some of you may still be pinning your hopes on that big Lotto win or planning on doing nothing yet because you'll inherit sooner or later anyway. If you are spending all you have whilst waiting for 'the big one', the chances are very high that, even if a sudden large windfall landed in your lap, you wouldn't be able to hold onto it for very long. If you know nothing else but spending what you earn, it may take you a little longer to spend a sudden large gain, but that is what you will do.

Unless good habits, such as planning, self-discipline and visualising your goal are firmly in place, that 'fortune' will diminish until you have nothing to show but the nice new toys and baubles you acquired. Even if you do believe that big win is just around the corner you may as well get into some good habits, just in case you do hit the jackpot.

The habit of absorbing extra income, such as pay rises or overtime payments, into your weekly spending is equally damaging to your financial future. This habit is very common. Remember, if it is that easy to increase your spending by 10 per cent, it is equally easy to reduce your spending by 10 per cent, if you are motivated enough to do it. After a while you don't notice the adjustment, but your bank account will.

This applies to the paying out of loans. Imagine that you have just paid off a personal loan. What do you do with repayments now? If you do nothing your spending will rise to absorb the repayment amounts. If you add the repayments to your current home loan without missing a beat, you will not have the chance to get used to the increase in your available income. Things will seem the same to you. To your bank, things will be looking a little less profitable. You have just speeded up your mortgage expiry date by several years and saved thousands of dollars in interest payments.

Holding on to it

All the qualities and habits for successful asset building that we have considered so far will be needed to hold on to windfalls and increases in available income, or they will just get lost in your spending.

You must visualise and live your goal. Plan how you will reach it and schedule dates for achieving each stage of it. Be persistent and strong-minded in the face of discouragement and criticism from those who know no better. Seek the company and the experience of like-minded people, or people who are already at the point you want to be. Be prepared to expend effort and maintain self-discipline. Act now and keep working on your goal every day in some way or another. Whether you are starting with 20 cent pieces or a windfall of many thousands of dollars, if you practise the six steps outlined at the beginning of this chapter with conviction and ambition, you *will* achieve your goal of financial independence.

If we look back at the examples in this chapter of family financial planning and compare how each will fare on retirement, the effectiveness of the six steps and the importance of financial intelligence becomes very obvious.

Which yearly income would you rather live on?

USING OTHER PEOPLE'S MONEY TO MAKE YOUR OWN!

n the previous chapter the concept of leverage and the process of increasing your investment earnings by increasing your borrowing were examined. In order to borrow money from a financial institution, you need to reassure them that you have both the ability to pay it back and a security behind you that they can cash in if things get desperate.

Lending institutions do tend to favour lending money for secure investments, such as property, but will also lend you money to buy shares and units in managed funds as well. If you are looking to invest in shares or managed funds, they will not lend you as much of the percentage value. A rough guide would be that the lending body will lend you anything from 80 to 100 per cent of your available equity for property and 50 to 70 per cent for other investments.

This is why I have always gone for property investments. I know the bank will give me what I need to use the power of leverage. I also do not have to face the fear of margin calls.

Margin lending and margin calls

If you are borrowing without equity in your own home, the banks and other institutions will often allow you to borrow money directly against the shares or units you want to buy. This 'margin lending' means that you do have to put some money of your own in. A common example is where you put in 30 per cent and the lending body puts in 70 per cent. As you probably already are aware, shares go up and down. Over time they do even out and do give excellent returns, but lending bodies tend to get a bit nervous when they fall below the value of what they have lent you to buy them in the first place.

At this point you will normally receive a margin call, an order from the lending body to either top up the value of your investment from your own pocket or to let them sell shares or managed funds units in order to cover the fall in value. This can be catastrophic. The worst time to sell is when the price is falling. The bank makes sure it won't lose its money, but you do not have that luxury.

Check also what loan fees apply with margin lending. They can be quite expensive. If this is the only way you can borrow money then check it out thoroughly. Talk to a financial planner or adviser. Talk to people who have done it before. Do your research before you approach a margin lender. Diversify your shares or share funds. When one lot goes down in value, the losses can often be offset by another lot going up in value. Reinvest your dividends or distributions to increase your percentage of ownership or equity. Margin lending is not for the faint-hearted, but it can be better than nothing if it is done wisely and with full awareness of the consequences of a sustained or dramatic fall in the market.

In chapter 5, the different options for investment in equity assets, (assets you then own part or all of) are covered in more detail. The main point here is that, with a little care and a lot of planning and forethought, even if you do not own your own home, you can borrow money on the security of shares or managed funds you might already have, or want to buy. Not, perhaps, as much as you can borrow with equity in your own home and not as much as if you were looking to buy investment property, but it may be better than nothing.

However you manage to secure the fund you need, one thing is sure, you will be paying interest to the lending body for the privilege of spending their money. There are a range of loans and loan packages that might suit you. Do your research, talk to different lending bodies. Explain what you need and what you are going to do with it. If you are panic-stricken by the thought of interest rates rising, you can lock into a fixed interest loan. If you want to keep your ongoing investment costs down to a minimum, an interest-only loan may be the way to go. Interest-only loans, as in the examples of property investment in the previous chapter, mean that you can get on with reducing the debts you already have whilst paying only the interest on the new debt, at a fixed rate.

More on interest–only loans

Once you have got rid of your previous debts, you may then choose to change your interest-only loan to the sort of loan you probably have on your own home, the principal and interest loan. In this way you will begin to pay off not just the interest, but also the principal part of your loan, so reducing your interest payments as you go. Or you may decide to keep paying just the interest for some years. This has the advantage of allowing inflation to eat into the real dollar value of the money you owe and allowing your equity in the investment to go up through capital growth alone. The money you were paying on the debt you have just wiped out can go to further investment, so increasing your investment earnings for the future. Then you might decide to sell the assets on retirement and pay the principal amount back as a lump sum.

Let's put some hypothetical figures into action here, to illustrate the possibilities of interest-only loans. If we assume you are going to buy an investment property with an interest-only loan of $420,000, currently fixed for five years at 7.6 per cent, you will be paying $31,920 each year in interest. That's $614 a week. It sounds a lot, but consider also the rent and the tax rebates and you will probably, if you are earning an income of $50,000 a year gross, end up paying $40-$70 a week to hold the property. If we take the inflation rate as an average of 4 per cent a year over this five-year period and capital growth at a 6 per cent rate, then, at the end of five years the property will be worth around $600,000 and the real value of the money you have borrowed will have gone down to $344,400. Your equity has gone up, you now own $180,000 of the property. If your wages have kept pace with inflation, your real dollar value of debt will have actually dropped, without you paying any of the principal amount back!

Now you lock in the loan for another five years of interest-only at 9.6 per cent (assuming interest rates move upwards). You will be paying $775 a week in interest. However, as your income has gone up, so has your tax, and so will your rebates! Your rent will have gone up too! So you may still be paying a few dollars a week to hold the property. In the meantime, a capital growth of 6 per cent means your property will have increased in value to around $800,000. Inflation at 4 per cent means the real dollar value of the $420,000 you borrowed has dropped to $281,400!

You lock in again for another five years at, let's say, 10.75 per cent interest. Inflation is still (miraculously!) 4 per cent and capital growth has (also strangely!) stayed at a low 6 per cent. At the end of this five years, your property will be worth around $1,000,000, of which $580,000 is yours. The interest payments have gone up to $868 a week. Your rent and your wages will also have gone up too! You will probably be 'positively geared' by now, actually making a profit of a few dollars a week, after all expenses have been taken out. The real dollar value of the original $420,000 loan is now $235,200!

So you sell, pay back the original $420,000 and pay the capital gains tax and selling costs of around $189,000. This leaves you with a total profit of $391,000. The cost to you in holding the property in the early years was, perhaps, a total of around $5,000. It is also possible that it all evened out from being first negatively and then positively geared over the 15 years and so cost you nothing!

Consider also what happens if inflation goes up more. Your rents and your wages will also rise more. The real dollar value will drop further. If capital growth goes up past 6 per cent, you will be laughing! Your equity in the property will get bigger and bigger, giving you more profit at the end, when you sell it!

Let's play devil's advocate now. If by some strange turn of events, inflation was to drop and stay dropped, the real dollar value of the principal you borrowed would not drop as much, but that makes no difference to your everyday outgoings and incomings. Your wages and rents would also not rise as much. Since you have a fixed rate of interest, this should not affect you, since you have calculated you can manage your repayments at the beginning of the five-year period. A rise in wages would have been a nice bonus, but you are not dependent on it to keep up with the fixed interest payments.

What if interest levels went up to 18 per cent? Well, you have time on your side, since you have fixed your rate for five years and there is a very good chance the interest rate will have started to drop before you have to renegotiate the interest rate with the lending institution again. If it really got too much, you would have time to sell the property and pay out the loan at the end of the five year fixed period.

What if capital growth slowed down? If you have chosen a premium property in the first place (see chapter 7 for more information on premium property) then I doubt very much that it would affect your property to the point when it would start to go backwards in value. If property prices did start dropping, you still have that fixed period to weather out the fall in value.

By going through these possibilities, I hope I've demonstrated that, with commitment, with resilience and with a well-informed approach, risk in investment becomes manageable and your perception of the risk becomes more realistic. Investment is for realists. Optimists gamble and pessimists do nothing!

Anyway, back to the main point! Using money you haven't got yourself is a quick way to building your investment portfolio. This is best suited to the financially intelligent, since it needs planning, research, commitment to saving and courage. The rich get richer and stay that way because of financial intelligence, not through luck or a doctorate in systems analysis.

Whose assets are they anyway?

An important consideration in investing is whose name should the assets be in. This is important. All of the successful property investments I have set up use tax legislations to reclaim money for me from the ATO as I go. Without this, it would be much harder for me to afford my investments. We have been looking at tax-effective investments, because, as long as the investment is in the right name, a sizeable part of your weekly tax can be diverted into paying off your own investment for the future.

In the case of shares, for example, shares that are already 'franked' have been taxed once by the government before you buy them. So when you buy them, some or all of that franking will come back to you as a tax refund. Great, but what if you are unemployed or the shares are in your partner's name, and he or she does not earn enough to be taxed? Then there is no refund.

If you have borrowed money to buy shares or units in a managed fund you can claim back some of the borrowing costs, such as interest on the loan, bank fees, brokerage fees and fund management fees. Again, if one partner is not paying tax or paying very little tax, it would be financially better for the partner earning more to have these assets in their name only, because then they can get the full tax refunds.

What if you and your partner buy an investment property and, in these days of equality, you decide that, even though you earn 70 per cent of the household's income, the property should go jointly into both names? This means that you can only claim tax refund on half your expenses and your partner may find he or she doesn't pay enough tax to actually get back all of the refund they are entitled to. If their tax bill for the year is $4,000 and they are entitled to refunds of $8,500, they will only get the $4,000. This is $4,500 that you have missed out on. And who said romance isn't dead? It isn't dead, but it can be expensive when it comes to investment! If you have a large chunk of money taken out of your pay packet each week and your partner only pays a few dollars each week, it is far more sensible in financial terms to have the property in your name only. That way all of the refund entitlement will come back to you through a refund or reduced weekly tax rate.

Be aware, a profitable investment property, share portfolio or managed fund can push you up to the next tax bracket. You may just have to chalk that up to the cost of success! In many cases you do have the option of transferring deeds of ownership and assets across to your partner, but this costs money in legal fees, stamp duties, capital gains tax and possibly other charges. If you are not sure if this is a worthwhile option, talk to your accountant. It may be cheaper to stay put.

Generally speaking, if you have borrowed money to buy equity assets and they are negatively geared, it is better to have them in the name of the highest earner.

The opposite could apply if you have interest-bearing assets such as term deposits or bonds. These, if put into the name of the highest tax payer, could move them up to a higher tax bracket and will certainly be taxed at the tax payer's highest rate. Interest-bearing investments may not be tax-effective for higher income earners. If you are getting 6 per cent interest on your investments and then being taxed 48.5 per cent on this 6 per cent, your effective return is 3.1 per cent If inflation is around 3 per cent you are not exactly making a sizeable profit on these types of investment. Put these investments into the name of a low-income or no-income earner and the interest will either be taxed at a much lower rate or not be taxed at all.

If you are worried about the inequality of ownership on paper, update your will so that it becomes clear where you want the assets to go after you have died. If your partner is worried about what might happen with division of assets if the relationship or marriage did not last, an agreement can be drawn up with your solicitor to clarify how, in fact, the assets will be divided in the case of separation or divorce.

ARTCHA '02

If both partners are earning similar wages then joint ownership may be the way to go. Joint ownership of assets means that the assets are held equally by those named and so, for tax refund or rebate purposes, each will be eligible for 50 per cent of the total entitlement. If one of those named in joint ownership dies, ownership of the assets automatically passes to the survivor on the titles.

If you want both partners' names on the titles of property assets, for romantic, egalitarian or whatever reasons, then joint tenancy may be an option. Unlike joint ownership, joint tenants can nominate split ownerships up to 99 per cent to 1 per cent. In which case you will have to lodge a partnership tax return each year and you will need to ensure you have updated your wills.

Other options of asset ownership, such as family trusts, companies, partnerships and syndicates, also exist and may suit different situations, such as assets held by groups of investors who have pooled together to buy a property or a share portfolio or assets held by families. Your accountant and solicitor will have the relevant information if you want to follow these options up. Different options will have different legal, financial and tax considerations, so tread carefully before making a decision. If you are simply looking for the best option for you and your partner, then individual or joint ownership, or joint tenancy will probably be the simplest and most effective solution. If your situation is less than simple, talk to the experts. An unwise decision may cost you dearly.

Get rich quick schemes and other disasters!

Speaking of unwise decisions, now may be a good time to look at frauds, scams and other misdemeanours. A friend of mine recently told me about a cute little scam that his mother encountered a few months ago. She received a letter that told her that her name had been drawn, at random, out of thousands of names and she was a WINNER! She had won a cash prize, which, once the draw was complete, would be forwarded to her in the near future. However, if she wished to receive this prize within a couple of weeks, all she needed to do was to send a cheque for $30 to PO Box 462 ... His mother thought it was extremely funny and very cheeky! Luckily!

The sad part of this is that, although we may laugh, how many people actually did send money to these tricksters? And how many of them, do you think, received a cash prize? These schemes operate constantly and prey on the isolated, the vulnerable, the desperate and the trusting. By the time these people realise that there is no cash prize, or, if there is, it's a dollar coin taped to a 'thank you' note, it's too late. The post office box has been closed. The schemers have moved on and will do it again after the dust has settled.

Chance of a lifetime?

You might think you would never be that stupid! Think again. A slightly more sophisticated scam was worked in the mid-eighties. It was pitched at investors who had replied to a mail-out offer of a free investment newsletter. The newsletter seemed legitimate. It had share and stock reports and forecasts for many legitimate companies across the globe. Some were relatively new. One was featured in the newsletter over three months. Its share prices rose and rose. Then the phone calls began, offering a limited purchase of US$5,000 to first-comers on this about-to-be floated company. It was based in an obscure country in Europe.

How do you trust someone from an overseas broking firm who you've never heard of and who tries to sell you shares over the phone in a company you have no proof actually exists? Several millions of US dollars and thousands of red-faced investors later... guess what! The company that was to be the making of their fortunes did not actually exist!

Another scam that arrived on my doorstep a few weeks ago, was in the form of a fax from General Mumbutu. He proclaimed himself as a 'retired' military leader in Nigeria and claimed that he had sold a cache of diamonds that he had 'skillfully and cleverly accumulated' whilst his regime had been in power, and he now needed to bank $25,000,000 overseas! Please could he use my bank account to transfer the cash? He would let me keep 10 per cent for my trouble! If I was interested in making $2,500,000 then I needed to send him my bank account details and number, but I would have to be quick, because he was operating on a 'first come, first served' basis!

Scams come in many forms and all work along the same lines. They promise you either something for nothing or the opportunity to get rich quick. They use hooks to snare the gullible, the financially unintelligent, such as 'outstanding returns', 'no capital needed', 'a simple and fast way to get rich'. The only people who do get rich quick are the instigators of these scams. There is a simple equation that applies to investments.

The higher the returns, the higher the risk

For returns that are exceptionally high, the risks go through the roof. The scams all work on the financially unintelligent, the people who are lazy, greedy, want something for nothing – or are naïve and gullible. I repeat, the higher the returns, the higher the risk. For would-be investors, I'm tempted to ask them to write out that line one hundred times before they part with their dollars!

Here are some names that promised huge returns to their investors; Quintex, Hooker Corporation, Budget Corporation, Bond Corporation. What they didn't promote was the huge risk. As many shareholders found, the high returns disappeared into nothing once these corporations got into trouble. In 1990 Estate Mortgage ran television and glossy print advertisements (all paid for by investors' money!) that promised returns up to 5 per cent higher than other similar investment schemes. They were offering 17 per cent returns and getting a 2 per cent annual fee. In other words, they were lending out their investors' money at 19 per cent interest. What property developer would go to them to borrow at 19 per cent interest when the banks were offering around 15 per cent? Simple. Those developers whose projects were too risky for the banks to touch. Many of the projects failed and Estate Mortgage collapsed in 1991. Tens of thousands of investors lost part or all of their money that year.

The Queensland Bite!

There is another type of scam operating that does not work through promising you huge returns and underplaying or ignoring the corresponding risk. It works through selling investment properties at a much higher price than they are worth. It has been operating in various forms since the late eighties and is legal, insofar as that if you are selling a property it is accepted you will sell for as much as the buyer is willing to pay.

Imagine this. You receive a phone call from someone to tell you that you have been specially selected, (How? Where from?) to attend a seminar on wealth creation and property investment. If you ask them where they got your name from, they will often say that you have been referred by someone who attended the last seminar. (If, as I do, you say you are busy and ask them for their home phone number so that you can call them back later, they will normally hang up!) The seminar will cost you nothing. Sometimes there's even the bait of a prize to be drawn at the end of the seminar with all attending eligible to participate! Yes, you too can get something for nothing!

Assuming they get you there, you may be plied with wine and food whilst they deliver a slick and impressive script on the benefits of investing in new developments, mainly in Queensland, and mainly in or around the Gold Coast, Sunshine Coast and Brisbane. The benefits of negative-gearing, capital growth and rental income are extolled. It works, because they are actually basing all of this on facts. They cap it off with an offer of a free or greatly discounted airfare for you and your family to fly up and take a look. Tempting, yes? Surely it's worth taking a look? I mean, the free trip to sunny Queensland is hard to resist. And you're hooked!

They haven't landed you yet, though. So off you go to Queensland. You are met at the airport and whisked off to a day of sight-seeing, property-inspecting and the establishment of golden dreams of prosperity and riches. All the properties they take you to look at are new, beautifully landscaped, with great facilities, pools, parks, tennis courts and potentially huge capital growth. After a day of being escorted through properties you are taken to the company's offices and then the pressure begins. You're probably tired and overwhelmed by the day's touring. They tell you that only a few properties are remaining and they are selling so fast that it's important for you to place a deposit now. It would be awful if you had to miss out because you couldn't make up your mind. You are being given the 'hard-sell'.

At this point many people sign on the dotted line and return to their home States exhausted, confused and a little apprehensive. At this point the company directors are rubbing their hands with glee! Yet another property sold at $30,000 or more mark-up on its true market value. On this whirlwind tour, you were not given the time to look in estate agents' windows, let alone get an independent valuation on the property or find out about the rental potential or capital growth of similar properties in the area. The company knows that if you are allowed to go back home and think about it, they have lost their catch of the day. You may have swallowed the hook, but you've broken the line and they have lost you.

For those caught, all seems to be going smoothly until they try to sell the property, or they get a different valuation from the one the company provided – and discover that they have been overcharged by tens of thousands. In some cases people have paid more than a hundred thousand over what they discover their property is worth.

How does this work? You know how much your own house is worth. You are probably aware of how much houses in your local area are selling for. Let's say you live in Sydney or Melbourne. Once you have been flown up to Queensland, you are disoriented. You have no local knowledge, you have no ides of local prices, but everything seems so cheap, compared to your home city. It's all new and sparkling. Then the confusion and exhaustion of a whirlwind tour begins. Tiredness and stress often make us do stupid things. The hard-selling at the end of the day is far more effective on a person who is tired, emotional and overwhelmed by facts and figures, all geared to push you into saying, "Yes! I'll take it!"

The company, because of the huge profits they make, only have to sell a few hundred properties a year to be laughing all the way to the bank. The seminars bring in tens of thousands of prospective investors each year, so, they only need to net a very small percentage of seminar-attenders to make this work. It's usually all legal, but nonetheless to my mind it's still 'criminal'. Before you buy any property, insist on an independent valuation, a cooling off period and time to do your homework on its investment potential.

In my line of business I'm often called on to help people sort out the mess they have found themselves in. One example comes to mind of a couple who shall remain nameless! They had been swept off their feet at a seminar, flown free of charge to the Gold Coast, pressured to sign up for an investment property – a townhouse on a new estate inland from the Gold Coast. The couple bought it for $180,000. When they could not get the rent they expected, they approached a local estate agent for help. They found the property was valued on the local market at just over $60,000! After talking to me, they sold it for $65,000 and carried forward the $115,000 loss to offset the capital gains tax on the future sale of the Sydney CBD property they then bought with my help. Capital losses can be carried forward to either very profitable years, to bring down the tax bill, or, as with this couple, to the point at which they sell and are liable for capital gains tax on their profits from the Sydney property.

That time of year again!

There is also the scam that takes advantage of panic and desperation. More investment schemes are publicised and advertised at the end of the tax year than in all the rest of the year put together. It is easy to understand why. For those who need to 'spend' part of their income in a way that they can then claim it as a sizeable tax deduction and so reduce their tax bills, these timely adverts are very alluring.

The investment schemes they promote vary in product, from macadamia nuts to yabbies, from protea to feature films. The ventures advertised need capital. They are aimed at those who need to spend capital to reduce their tax liabilities. The ventures boast of great returns and excellent rates of capital growth. The companies running them play down or forget to mention the high risks associated with the investments. The investors are in too much of a hurry to sign the paperwork and get it all to their accountants before the end of June to do much research on what they are actually investing in. How much does the average investor know about running a macadamia plantation or about emu farming? These schemes operate on the haste and panic of the ill-prepared and uninformed investor. As with the Queensland property schemes, they take advantage of a stressed and confused state of mind. Investment can be likened to getting married. Invest in haste, repent at leisure!

The typical tax scheme will arrange finance for you, enabling you to borrow. Many have higher rates of interest than you would get from your own bank. Your own bank would probably be very cautious about lending you money for many of these schemes, deeming them to be of very high risk. In the first year, you will be able to claim on the initial outlay immediately. If you invest $10,000 and are in the $60,000-plus income bracket, you will be able to claim a tax refund of 48.5 per cent of the amount you have paid out to the nut plantation or emu farm. Your rebate of $4,850 sounds good, but, if the project fails, the whole exercise will have cost you $5,150. If it makes it past the first year (and over 60 per cent of small businesses fail in the first year) then you will be able to claim back the interest payments you have paid out on your loan. All you are getting back is what you have paid out in the first place. Unless these rebates drop you into a lower tax bracket, your net profit is nothing.

Some, but only some, of these ventures may work out. Many others are no longer operating by the end of the third year, just when they were supposed to be starting to make a profit for the investors, or, at least, breaking even. This means that your total gain in tax dollars is about half of what you borrowed in the first place. This does not strike the financially intelligent as a scheme worth getting involved with.

Another bad reason to get involved with such investments is emotional loading. Just because you happen to love yabbies is no good reason to put your money into a new yabby farm. You may a fan of, or even know a famous person in films – but no matter how popular the star or the director, the box-office success of films is as hard to predict as the weather. Nearly two-thirds of the films made for general release worldwide end up on video release only. Some don't even make it that far.

So what can the panic-driven investor do to lessen the tax bill at the end of the year if emus and echinacea are not the answer? They could always do what the financially intelligent investor would do and take out an equity loan to buy shares, managed funds or property and prepay the interest for the following year before the end of June. All costs and any interest prepaid will then be deducted from their taxable income, thus reducing their tax bill. After this they can sit back, keep claiming rebates on interest payments and costs and watch their investments grow and grow over time, until the time comes to sell them and pay back the original loan.

How can we evaluate the integrity of investment schemes and systems? It is simple to check an investment opportunity's credentials. Talk to people who are already investors wherever possible. Many scheme promoters can provide you with written testimonials, but you will learn far more from talking directly to existing investors. If the company or corporation administering the scheme cannot or will not give you contacts for existing investors, either look elsewhere or talk to independent financial planners and brokers, who can do some research for you. At least they can give you information concerning the previous performances of the investment products you are interested in. If you are interested in a new venture that cannot give you records of past performance, find information on similar ventures in similar climates or environment and use their performance as an indicator of what might happen.

Key points in evaluating the integrity of investment schemes and systems

A good investment option will have certain features:

- A 'get rich slowly' approach
- A clear indication of how long you will need to leave your money there to get the best possible returns
- A clear explanation of your responsibilities
- An indication of the risk level you are laying yourself open to
- A record of past performances, where applicable
- A clear and reasoned forecast of future performances, where possible
- Testimonials and contacts for existing investors (although this will probably not be possible with shares, managed funds and other large business investment schemes)
- An invitation to attend AGMs and other meetings, where appropriate
- Cooling off periods, where appropriate
- Regular feedback and updates of information on the schemes or products you have invested in

A financially intelligent investor will also have certain features!

- A clear goal to aim for, expressed in terms of how much and when by
- A strong motivation and desire to achieve the goal
- A clear step by step plan to reach the goal
- Commitment and energy to proceed with the plan
- Self-control and restraint
- Contacts with experienced and successful investors, financial planners and other experts in the field

- The ability to research and gather information
- The self-confidence to stand by decisions
- An understanding of the levels of risk the investor is comfortable with
- Courage and conviction to ward off the negative influences of others who do not understand or practise financial intelligence.

Which one shall we get this year?

C H A P T E R   5

THE OPTIONS
AVAILABLE IN THE
INVESTMENT MARKET

I n a consumer-dictated society we are faced with an almost overwhelming range of choices in even the simplest product. Take toilet
rolls, for example. Next time you are at your local supermarket count
how many options are available to you! Two-ply, three-ply, perfumed,
hypoallergenic, quilted, patterned, pastel-coloured, bleached, unbleached,
economy, luxury and more! Investment options can sometimes seem just
as overwhelming. It is not my intention to do more than outline the
main investment options and look at their comparative advantages and
disadvantages. Books are on the market that specialise in just one type of
investment – so more detailed information is available to you once you
have decided which type of investment suits you and your goals and
financial plans.

Which investment works best for you is controlled by certain parts of
your individual investor profile. Some of the characteristics of this profile
must be considered. A key factor is age. If you are 21 you may risk
choosing a more volatile investment than if you are 61, as you'll have
more time to even out the ups and downs of an investment that may give
you negative as well as positive returns. If you are looking for fast capital
growth at this stage of your life, rather than generating larger investment

incomes, then such investments as bonds, debentures and fixed interest investments may not be your ideal choice.

If you react badly to risk, even managed risk, and find it difficult to relax with the thought that your investments may slide backward as well as jump forward then shares may not be the answer for you.

If you are currently renting and are saving up for a deposit to enable you to buy your own home, you might be better off focusing all your savings in a saving account with bonus interest paid whenever the deposits outweigh the withdrawals or a high-interest savings account that allows you to access your money without forfeiting your first-born child.

If you are paying income tax and own your own home, or have paid off at least some of it, then you may be able to borrow to buy other assets such as investment properties or a shares portfolio, or even units in a managed fund. Such assets will not only boost your capital growth values but will also result in some worthwhile tax deductions in your favour. In some cases tax deductions are a nice little bonus, in other cases tax issues are a major consideration in taking on such a loan. As we look at the options available to us for investment we need to take such factors into account to enable us to make the right decisions at the right times.

Imagine you are about to place a bet on a horse in the Melbourne Cup. There is no point backing a sprinter over a long course. It would be a waste of money to put money on a horse that doesn't like heavy going – when it's been raining for a week and the forecast predicts more rain on the day. The chances of the horse doing well with a jockey who has never ridden the course or ridden the horse before are less than with an experienced jockey who is familiar with the animal. It might be fun to choose a horse just because you like the look of it or its name, but it isn't a good way to maximise the prospects of making money on your wager.

In the same way people need to consider such factors before putting their hard-earned money into investments. If interest rates are on the way down, perhaps now is not the time to lock your money into a fixed-interest investment. If you are going to trust your investment planning to a financial adviser who is fresh out of college and is only just starting up, perhaps you should let other investors break him or her in before you climb on board. This also applies to investing in shares. If you want solidity and as low a risk as possible with your share selection you will probably go for the tried and tested, rather than put your money into a new company with no track record and no form.

The same could be applied to managed funds. If the fund has only

been in existence for three months, it is difficult to come up with accurate performance projections. I mean, it's hard enough when the funds
have been going for five years or more! (Notice that every single
prospectus for a managed fund states that the fund's past performance is
no indication of its future performance. The fund promoters have put
that in, not because of a strong sense of social conscience, but because
they have to. Otherwise their material can be deemed misleading and
possibly even fraudulent.) The past does not equal the future in fund
management, any more than it does in share performances, but, at least
with some sort of track record in front of you, you are able to increase
your odds of picking the right horse for the right course.

Equity-based versus Interest-based

To begin with we can divide the field into two broad sections. The
first section being equity-based investments and the second section being
interest-based investments. Broadly speaking, equity assets provide capital
growth and dividends, distribution payments or rent. They are based on
you, the investor, actually owning a part (or, eventually, all, in the case of
investment properties) of the company or other investment product you
have invested in. Vehicles for investment include shares, property, managed
funds, listed and unlisted property trusts and superannuation funds.

Interest-bearing investments are based on loans to financial institutions such as banks, governments, mortgage companies, insurance companies and unlisted companies. The idea is, you lend them the money for
their development, debt reductions or their own investment plans – and
they pay you back the money at a set time with interest that may be
fixed or may be variable according to the type of investment. The products available include government bonds, bank bills, cash management
trusts, debentures and unsecured notes. Interest-bearing assets normally
give no option for capital growth and generally give lower returns than
equity-based assets. They are, however, seen as having fewer surprises and
less volatility than equity assets.

If you buy a government bond for $10,000 for a five-year term, you
know the government has guaranteed you will get back exactly that, as
well as accrue some extra money through interest payments along the
way. These interest payments will be predictable and can either be taken
out or can be compounded as you choose. If you buy $10,000 worth of
shares in a major company, five years down the track they may be worth

$13,500 or $9,500. The dividends they earn cannot be forecast with any accuracy either. The only thing you can be sure of with shares is that they will go up and down, but over the long term they generally outperform any other investment option on the market.

Some of the 'equity' investments mentioned above actually have a component of both equity and interest based in the same product. Most managed funds and superannuation funds offer fixed-interest, interest-bearing and cash segments in some of their composite, off-the-shelf fund structures. The mix of these components is chosen to lower volatility of equity-based products by diluting them with interest-bearing products. They also offer interest-bearing only packages for those investors with a great need for low risk, conservative environments and equity-based only packages for those who want exposure to the higher returns (and risks) of the equity markets. The fund managers of some super funds have also incorporated a do-it-yourself product in their prospectuses. The investor can design their own package from the core components on offer by the fund and choose what ratio they hold these components in.

So let's outline the form of the main runners in the equity-based investment field.

Shares. Buying shares is becoming more popular in Australia as more companies have been floated on the stock market to which 'ordinary' people can subscribe without going through a stockbroker. For example, Telstra, Commonwealth Bank of Australia and NRMA. The act of share-buying and the state of being a shareholder has to a large extent been demystified and made accessible to all. There has been a rise in the number of 'mum and dad' investors in the share market over the last few years and this has been indicated by the percentage of Australians owning shares nearly doubling in the four years to 1998 to more than 28 per cent. This figure did not include the shares held indirectly through managed funds and super funds. If these are included the percentage of Australians owning shares in 1998 was over 40 per cent. This has made Australia the second biggest share-investing nation after the United States. (Figures from the Australian Stock Exchange)

What is it that makes shares increasingly popular? For a start, you can invest in shares with only a few hundred dollars (although you won't be able to buy many, nor will you be able to diversify greatly. A few thousand dollars is a lot more effective). Increasing share awareness gives new meaning to the financial pages of your usual newspaper – and to that bit at the end of news bulletins where they discuss the ups and downs of financial markets! Some shareholders do prefer not to look, though!

Shares are very 'liquid'. If you want to buy or sell, this can be done almost immediately. They are flexible. You can buy or sell a small part, a large part or all of your shareholdings. They are easy to buy and sell through a stockbroker. To find one, talk to people you know who already use one, call the Australian Stock Exchange (ASX) for a list, or look in the phone book or on the ASX website. Or you can buy through a traders' site on the Internet. (See 'Useful Contacts' later in this book.)

Buying shares. There is a fee for buying shares, unless they are bought directly through a prospectus. This fee may be in the form of a percentage (around 2 to 3 per cent) of the total value of the shares you are buying, or may be a flat fee of around $50 to $90. If your broker wants to charge a flat fee, it makes sense to make sure you buy enough shares in one go to minimise the percentage that the broker's fee takes away from you. If you buy only $400 in shares and are paying a $50 fee, you are paying the broker 12.5 per cent of your investment. It is possible to shop around and to negotiate with a broker to make sure you pay as low a fee as possible. Some brokers will charge on an either/or basis. If a percentage fee is worth more to them than a flat fee, because of the number of shares you are buying, they'll charge you the percentage. If you are not happy, contact a few others and see what their rates and services are like. Discount brokers offer you a 'no frills' approach for a lower fee or percentage. These brokers offer no advice – they are simply the checkout operators, who take your money without commenting on what you are buying. On top of brokers' fees is a stamp duty. This is currently 0.3 per cent of the value of the shares (and may vary in each State).

The main reason shares are so popular is that over the long term (10 years or more) shares have been star performers in capital growth and income-generation. International shares have traditionally outperformed every other equity-based investment on the market, including Australian shares, which currently occupy less than 2 per cent of the total share market available to us for investment purposes.

Pick and mix? Shares are available in many different sectors, including mining and heavy industry, financial industries and banks, technology and development industries, service industries, such as health, transport and tourism, and retail industries. The safe investor would probably invest in a mixture of shares from different sectors wherever possible. If one part of the economy slumps, hopefully other parts will maintain or increase their values to compensate. This is, of course, based on the old adage of not putting all your eggs in one basket. I would advise that quality is a crucial factor. Quality in shares can be identified by a little homework or 'due diligence' on the company or service provider you are buying into. For example:

• Get copies of the annual reports. Larger companies may have investor relations departments, smaller companies may have shares departments or ask to speak to the company secretary. If they know you are looking at buying shares in their company and are not very helpful at this stage, I'd give them a miss anyway, since they obviously do not value their potential shares investors highly enough. If you are put off by the person that answers the phone, think about how a prospective client of the company might feel at such treatment. They would probably feel less than enthusiastic too and might take their business elsewhere.

• Ask the company for a record of dividend payments. How long have they been paying ordinary dividends to their shareholders? If there are big gaps in their dividend payment records, I'd give it a miss. It might reflect either a lack of profits to pass on or poor money management.

• Ask the company (or your stockbroker) for the Barcep consensus figures of analysts' predictions and expectations of profits, earnings and dividends per share for the current year and the following year.

• If the company is based in your home city, visit them and attend the Annual General Meeting (AGM), if possible.

• Does the foyer in company headquarters reek of expensive fittings and more marble and fountains than a cultural tour of Rome? Maybe this company is spending too much of its money on trying to impress! On the other hand, if the HQ is in a somewhat sleazy-looking area, up nine flights of badly lit stairs, with no lift and more cockroaches than staff in the reception area, I'd question whether the company is making any money at all!

• Read investment periodicals. 'Personal Investor' has lists of the top 300 shares. The ASX journal, a monthly journal, shows share performances over one and three year periods. This is an interesting and informative resource that can help you make a decision, but, again, do not read too much into past performances. They are just that, past, and are no guarantee of asset behaviour in the future.

How are shares taxed? There is a tax consideration to be made on purchasing shares. When you buy the average share, it will be 'franked'. What this means is that the company issuing them has already paid company tax on its profits at (the current rate of) 36 per cent. When the company issues dividends on these shares you will only have to pay tax on the dividends if your marginal tax rate is higher than the company tax rate of 36 per cent. Then you will pay tax on the dividend payments at the tax rate that equals the difference between your marginal rate and company tax rate. In other words, if you are on 48.5 per cent marginal rate, you will only have to pay tax on your dividend earnings of 48.5 per cent minus 36 per cent, which is a tax rate of 12.5 per cent (because the government has already taxed the profits before they left the company and got to you).

If you sell your shares and they have gone up in value since you purchased them you will be liable to a tax called 'capital gains tax' (CGT) which is applicable to all equity investments, property, managed funds, property trusts and super funds. For equity assets purchased from the end of 1999, once you have held them for over a year, this tax is worked out as the tax on the profits you have made on your equity assets after legitimate costs, such as brokerage fees.

Then, and here is another strategy by the government to encourage saving and investment, you will also be entitled to an option of only paying the tax on 50 per cent of your capital gains, so bringing the taxable amount down to half of the clear profit you have made on the equity investments. The other option is to forfeit the 50 per cent option and go for the profits to be index-linked to inflation. This could work in your favour if you have held the assets for over 10 years by the time you sell and inflation has been at a higher rate than it is now. Check it out with your accountant before you get to the stage of selling and they will work out for you the best option to choose.

People on no tax or very low marginal rates will not need to pay any tax on their dividends or earnings from equity assets. In fact the lower marginal tax payers may get an 'imputation credit' from the tax office to deduct from their normal income. (Obviously those who don't pay any tax won't get any use out of such a credit.) Even those at the highest rates can do well out of the dividend imputation system by paying less tax on their share than they would pay on their earnings from interest-based investments, such as bonds or deposits.

The one certainty in regard to shares! Whether you buy shares directly through a prospectus or a broker, or whether you buy them indirectly as a part of a managed fund or super fund, there is only one thing you can say with any certainty about shares – their values will fluctuate. If you are a worrier, this fluctuation can be the cause of stress and anxiety.

I have two solutions. One is, don't open your fund statements, put them in a drawer for five years and open them at the end of the five years, starting with the most current one! The other is – don't buy shares. If an investment plan containing a sizeable portion of shares is going to give you sleepless nights and premature grey hairs, you are sacrificing quality of life and contentment in the here and now for a few thousand extra when you retire. Not something I would recommend to anyone.

There are other ways to invest that may bring you in less capital growth and returns than shares, but will still ensure you have a comfortable and independent lifestyle once you stop working for a living. Shares investment is not the only runner in this race.

Managed funds are extremely popular because of their convenience, their competitiveness and the amount of choice they can offer the investor today. Using a managed fund, investors can pool relatively small amounts of money into a single fund, which then invests the pooled money in a range of investments (some funds ask for a minimum of $2,000 invested, others ask for $5,000).

As with shares, managed funds offer good liquidity, they are easy to sell and buy, and are flexible. You can add to your investments by direct debit on a monthly basis with most funds and transfer amounts into the funds from your bank account over the phone too!

From meek to aggressive. The investor can choose a fund they feel best suits them. The worriers and conservative investors can choose a very low risk fund with safe, but lower, returns on their money. The more aggressive and courageous can pick a package that incorporates moderate to high risk, with the consequent potential for moderate to high returns (and of course, the potential for moderate to high losses too).

The most conservative funds tend to favour interest-bearing investments, cash and short term securities, such as bank notes. More than half, perhaps even as much as 90 per cent of investors' money goes into these steady, stable income earners. Many of these types of funds offer a monthly or quarterly payment of 'distributions' – money earned by the investors on their total investment with the fund – to enable people to supplement their own incomes. Some even offer a guaranteed payment per quarter, regardless of how the investment is doing. If it achieves more than the guaranteed payment, the extra gets reinvested. If the fund does not perform as well as expected and the actual distributions don't meet the guaranteed payment, the difference gets taken out of your fund to make up the shortfall.

These funds are very useful for those who have retired and want to conserve their assets rather than focus on achieving capital growth and reinvesting any distributions to build up the total amount invested. The emphasis of these funds is on providing a regular income with low priority given to capital growth, in a low to very low risk environment. They will not make you rich, but they will maintain the value of your investments and provide perhaps a per cent or two in growth of value after inflation. If you were a horse, it would be the holding pen or stable of investment, rather than the open field or rolling hills. Not much room to turn around, but sheltered and predictable!

The returns and consequently the risks change with each of the available funds, normally as the equity proportion of the fund increases – until you arrive at funds that invest ninety per cent or more of the members' money in Australian shares, international shares, or a mix of the two. With these share-based funds you can participate in a wide-ranging shares portfolio investment without having to lay out tens of thousands of dollars. This gives you not only high capital growth potential, but also the coverage you need to lessen the risk of one share sector falling dramatically on the stock exchange. The higher return/higher risk end of the funds is aimed at longer-term investors, willing to put money in and hold on through ups and downs over five or more years. The emphasis of these funds is often on capital growth, rather than income-earning potential, as with the interest-bearing investment funds. Between these two extremes are the 'balanced' fund options that aim to provide a balance of capital growth and income-earning. I would weigh up how long you can tie your money up against the level of risk and return.

If you are two weeks away from retiring, it makes no sense to put your savings into a shares-based fund that needs five to eight years minimum to realise the full returns and capital growth. However, if you are 10 years younger, clear of debt and want to make your money work as hard as possible, then a capital growth biased fund with a higher level of return may be a very good option. Bear in mind that when you do retire, the money in one fund can be switched to another more conservative fund with the same fund provider for income provision – with no capital gains tax on the switched amount, unless the transaction generates a gain in the switch. If there is a loss of value through the switch, you are able to offset that loss against any capital gains tax you make from other sources in the same year. If you have no capital gains to offset the loss, you can carry this loss forward until you do have a capital gain you can offset it against, even if it is a number of years down the track.

Tax and the managed fund. Many funds offer a quarterly distribution of profits on members' investments and will credit them to a nominated account. For asset-building purposes, it is probably better to ask for these distributions to be reinvested automatically. If the aim of this investment is to grow assets, then redistribution is necessary to speed up the process of growth. If the distributions get put into your everyday bank account they will probably disappear in a tenth of the time it took to make the money. If they are reinvested, you can't miss what you never had and your investment grows much more quickly!

All profits made in the form of distributions to fund members are taxable as income. Any fund that involves investment in franked shares has the same tax rules on that part of the fund as direct ownership of shares will give you. In other words, if your marginal tax rate is lower than the company tax rate (currently 36 per cent), you may pay nothing and even get tax credits. If it is higher you only pay the difference in rates. Funds that have a portion of equity investments will also secure the same tax deal regarding capital gains tax (CGT) that directly owned shares get from the ATO for the equity-based portion of that fund. CGT is payable if you withdraw, transfer or switch any units from your fund. For more information talk to the ATO, a financial adviser or the fund provider.

What about membership fees? The fees vary. Some funds charge zero per cent entry fee and if you have had your investment for more than a certain number of years, zero exit fee. Some funds charge one to three per cent entry fee, but no exit fee. Others charge no entry fee, but do charge an exit fee. All funds charge a yearly management fee at various percentages. It is most common for these fees to be between one and two per cent of your total equity investment each year, depending on the type of fund and how much actual management the fund managers do. Some may be very active, others may have a more laid-back approach to management. Ask the fund's representative for more information on the fund's style of management and how they earn their management fees. You will be paying these fees – so you're the boss! Shares funds might be slightly higher, because of the increased work in monitoring and buying and selling large amounts of shares. Monthly income and income guarantee funds may also be higher because of the extra administration involved. Shop around. Funds who snare people with no entry or exit fees may have higher yearly management fees, so if you maintain the investments over many years, you may not be any better off.

Having mentioned the convenience of switching as your needs for income or your ability to cope with higher risks change, check to see if you will be hit with a switching fee before you sign up with one particular fund. It is certainly worth doing your homework here too. Fees and costs do vary enough to make a financial difference. There are so many funds to choose from that shopping around can be very advantageous. Read the fund prospectuses thoroughly. Talk to a financial adviser but be aware that many may receive commission from different funds – their recommendations may not be disinterested. Ask them about this. They have to disclose any such arrangements to you. Read investment periodicals. *Personal Investor* magazine has lists of funds and their performance figures, including a top-10 funds list over one, three and five years.

Many fund providers give percentage returns on their different funds that are based on reinvesting distributions. If you are looking for an income-earning facility from a fund and will not be reinvesting the distributions, you will need to be aware that the returns advertised in the glossy brochures and prospectuses may be less than shown. If in doubt call the fund provider or ask the financial manager. All prospective fund investors need to check those glossy brochures to see if the figures included are before or after the yearly management fees (MERs) have been deducted.

Superannuation funds. Almost all employed people are now invested in compulsory super funds, even if they are working part time or casual. Currently, the only exceptions to this are those who have been earning less than $450 a month, or the self-employed. Since 1999 the rules have changed a little and those earning between $450 and $900 a month can negotiate with their employers to have their superannuation contributions paid directly to them. I would only advise this if a few dollars a week is going to make or break the budget. The good thing about super contributions is that they are a form of enforced saving that you do not have to lift a finger to organise or budget for, since they come out of your pay packet before you get it. This good thing is also a bad thing when it comes to investing, since the money is locked up until you are at least 55 and unless you research your choice of super fund, the money may not be earning you as much as other opportunities for investment.

My general rule about investing in super funds is – until you are clear of debts and within 10 years of retirement, limit your contributions to super funds to those your employer puts in for you. The opportunity to 'top up' your super funds is best taken when you have paid off your home loan, when you have bought equities that are going to give you the returns and the growth you need to finance your retirement and when you have paid off your investment loan.

If you are self-employed it is up to you to make your own superannuation arrangements and the situation is quite different. Seek financial advice on this. You may well find it cheaper and more profitable to set up another type of investment fund, such as a managed share fund, with a direct debit or other form of regular contribution from your main bank account, rather than sign up with a super fund.

Taxing times. The tax situation of investing extra money in super is that your contributions are taxed at 15 per cent, unless they come from net (after tax) earnings, in which case there is no contributions tax.

If you have a facility at work called 'salary sacrificing', your employer can deduct extra money from your gross salary and pay it into the super fund for you, where it will be taxed at 15 per cent. This is a benefit if you are on a higher marginal tax rate than 15 per cent.

If you pay in money from your net (after you have been taxed) dollars you are, in fact, paying less of each gross (before you have been taxed) dollar than if you salary-sacrificed. Imagine you are on a 48.5 per cent marginal tax rate. $100 of your gross salary when invested through salary-sacrificing leaves you $85 that actually gets to your super fund. Without salary-sacrificing you are first taxed on that $100 at 48.5 per cent, leaving just over $51.50 available for investment in the fund.

When you are in a position to actually withdraw your super, the government will not tax you on these extra payments from net earnings, provided you withdraw the funds after you turn 55. If you take out any funds before you turn 55 (only through special dispensation from the government regulator in terms of proven hardship or suchlike), there is 20 per cent lump sum tax to be paid. This is one way of getting you to invest long-term! All your employer's contributions and your salary-sacrificed contributions (taxed at only 15 per cent) will be taxed at 15 per cent on withdrawal once you are over 55.

Dazed and confused? Many people are – and practise the ostrich manoeuvre as soon as super is mentioned. After all, the employer goes on making the contributions, the amount you have in the fund keeps getting invested – and hopefully gets bigger without you having to understand what is going on. However, thinking like an ostrich never made anyone wealthy! (When was the last time you saw an ostrich driving a Porsche?)

A little understanding and research could increase your super payout by thousands. If you succeeded in understanding the section on managed funds, then an understanding of superannuation is also within your reach. The only complications within this system are as the result of the government changing the rules several times (and probably changing them again). For example, post 1983 contributions are taxed on withdrawal at a different rate to pre 1983 contributions.

The first point I would like to make is that superannuation funds are *your* choice when it comes to extra contributions. Just because your employer uses one fund, does not mean you have to stick to it when it comes to adding your own contributions. If you terminate employment with a particular employer, you can roll-over the accumulated amount in the employer's super fund to your own choice of super fund. This should not cost you anything. There are many personal super funds in which those extra contributions or roll-overs may be invested. Research the available funds as you would a managed fund and you will be able to see what choices are available within each fund, what the expenses are for yearly management and the history of the fund's performances. Compare them to your employer's chosen fund and then make your choice. The younger you are, the more a percent or two will make a difference. If you are 25 and find a better fund for your money, it can make tens of thousands of dollars difference to your accumulated super funds by the time you retire.

I constantly ask people at seminars, "How many of you know what percentage return you received last year from your super fund?" Most people don't know. It's your money. You are paying someone to manage it for you. Find out what they are doing with it. Track the results annually. If you are not happy, change your fund. Roll your money over to a fund that gives you the returns you want.

The second point is that each fund has a range of investment choices at different levels of risk and return (as with the managed funds). If you are on the verge of retiring, it is probably a little late in the day to worry about that now. However, if there are still a few years to go, it is probably worth getting your money to work a little harder. If you have another 12 or more years to go before you throw away the alarm clock, you have time on your side and could risk a few ups and downs to get to the higher returns. Some funds charge a small fee to switch from one type of investment to another – some may charge $20, others charge nothing. Even if you open another fund for your own contributions and roll-overs, it is still worth looking at the possibility of changing investment types in your employer's fund.

Some funds even offer a 'design your own fund' option. You can select what makes up your investment portfolio. You choose the percent-age of shares, fixed interest, cash, property and other options for your money to be invested in. This is an interesting (and some might say enjoyable) challenge for the more confident and financially literate among us. It does give investors the option to say no to certain types of investment and promote the importance of others. Some may use this type of fund to create an equity-only fund, with no cash or fixed-interest investments. Others may go the other way and create something with no or very little equity.

Another pool of investment becoming popular with some investors is the socially responsible investments pool. Many fund providers (this is the case in managed funds too) give investors the option of investing in what they determine to be socially and ecologically responsible equities, such as shares and cash investments. Check with the funds as to how they define and screen socially responsible companies and projects. It will vary from fund to fund. These types of investment options are still in their infancy, but seem to be attracting enough investors to make them viable. One fund has given its 'Eco Pool' a long-term probability of a negative return as one year in every six years, the same as its 100 per cent Australian shares and 100 per cent international shares funds. Not surpris-ing really. The actual financial size of the fund is still quite low, because it is quite new and as with managed funds, the smaller the size of the fund, the more fluctuations get emphasised. It is also a 90 per cent shares/10 per cent cash fund and so is quite high on the risk/return chart.

The third point I would like to make about super funds is that many of us older people who have not been in a fund for all that long may want to top up our super funds with extra contributions. The time to top them up is when our money could not be more wisely spent on debt reductions or paying off loans more quickly. Achieve that first, then top up. This is far more effective a means of financial growth than leaving loans gathering interest because you want to invest in something.

When you look at where your money needs to be to make you better off, prioritise debt reduction – followed by equity-based investments that will give you capital growth as well as returns in the forms of dividends, distributions or rent. Interest-bearing investments, such as bonds or cash management trusts are best left until later in life, since these types of investments can generate a return through interest, but no capital growth. They are 'safer' than equities, because you are loaning money to a business to get interest and, as long as you choose a secured investment, you are guaranteed to get your initial investment back at the end of a set term. But on the whole, certainly over a long period of time, their returns cannot match those of equity-based investments.

Mature at last! Once you have reached retirement age there are several options to consider when it comes to taking out your money from super funds. If you need time to think, the best bet is to roll over your money into an approved super fund, an approved deposit fund or a deferred annuity. The money can stay there, gathering more returns until you are 65. It will still be taxed at the 15 per cent concessionary rate. You may then choose to buy from a range of annuities or pensions – but research them carefully. For information, ask experts, financial planners, retirement planners and those of your friends and family already retired who are using their super money.

If you take out your super to place it into a managed fund, or another form of investment not approved as a roll-over fund, you will be hit by the Lump Sum Tax! This can be as much as 15 per cent on all contributions made after 1983 that have not had contributions tax of 15 per cent paid (contributions before then will be taxed at 5 per cent). Net (after-tax) personal contributions are taxed at zero per cent.

You are taxed on all amounts above $100,000 (this is index-linked and with current trends would rise each year). This would be at 15 per cent for contributions that have already been taxed at the 15 per cent contribution tax rate when they went in, and at 30 per cent for the contributions that did not get taxed at any stage.

It is worth noting that as you get to the stage of topping up your super, you will find the amount you can invest each year through your employer or through salary-sacrificing is limited, depending on your age. Check with your super fund. The amount you can put in from your after-tax money is not limited. The amount you can accumulate is also limited by a Reasonable Benefits Limit (RBL), which is close to half a million dollars at present – something not many of us need to worry about just yet! Anything over the RBL is taxable at your highest marginal rate when you withdraw it as a lump sum.

Whole books have been written about superannuation, but this is not one of them! The rules change so often that every book I've read on the subject has a qualifier built in along the lines of 'These are the figures now, but there is no guarantee that the situation will be the same by the time you have finished this book!'

For up to the minute information, contact any superannuation fund or the Association of Superannuation Funds of Australia (ASFA).

Property Investment

Indirect property investment. Now we can talk about something that really interests me! Property investment can be broadly divided into two types, direct and indirect. Indirect investment is normally through specific property trusts or through a component of managed or super funds. This is a way of getting into property investment with small amounts of money. When it comes to property trusts there are two forms, listed and unlisted. Financial planners and stockbrokers can provide you with information and the relevant forms and prospectuses for investment in these trusts.

Both invest a pooled amount of money in ventures such as industrial property, commercial property and residential property and both give you the opportunity to spread your investments and so spread the risks. Like managed funds, you can go for income returns at the expense of capital growth and vice versa. Both are long-term investments and both give relatively more consistent and predictable gains than shares, although not always as high. Both may be a tax benefit to the investor through investment deductions and property depreciation costs, a small percentage of which are allowed as tax deductions. The tax situation will be covered in more detail in the section on direct property investments.

Buying units in listed trusts is like buying shares in property on the stock market. The listed trusts are in fact listed on the stock market and the units you buy act like ordinary shares. You even purchase them in the same way that you buy shares and sell them the same way too. The units in listed trusts even take on the same qualities of shares. The listed trusts offer more or less the same liquidity that shares do. The units behave in a more volatile (more up and down) fashion than those in unlisted trusts.

Unlisted trusts – far more common than their listed counterparts – are less liquid. You need to contact the trust manager and request to sell or redeem part or all of your unit holdings. This can take 60 days or more. The unlisted fund actually has to sell assets to pay out large amounts of units. If the trust is inundated with requests for redemptions of units, it can suspend redemptions for up to six months to give it a chance to sell assets in a way to protect the ongoing investors and the trust itself.

Imagine if property went into a decline, as it does do on a cyclic basis just as it goes into high returns on a cyclic basis – and many of the trust's investors got cold feet and wanted to redeem their units. The trust would be forced to sell assets just as they have reached a low point in their growth cycle. Thanks to the Australian Securities Commission, the trust is empowered to say to investors that they could wait up to six months before being paid out. This allows the market to pick up, or allows the trust to offer the units at a reasonable price to existing or new investors. (Personally I'm not that big on these forms of property investment. They rely too much on other people to succeed.)

As with managed funds and shares, if you sell units in property trusts you are subject to capital gains tax. As with dividends and distributions, your income returns from property trusts are deemed assessable income and so taxable by the ATO.

Another form of indirect investment is the property syndicate. This is a professionally managed syndicate with a registered prospectus that works on a smaller scale to the unlisted property trust. Because of a smaller pool of investors, the minimum investment is considerably higher than with property trusts. The range of properties invested in is also usually smaller as these syndicates may invest in only one or a few properties. The investments are also normally of a fixed term, often five or 10 years. There is also no obligation on the fund to buy back your units before the fixed term is over, although many will try to sell them on to other investors for you if you find yourself in financial hardship. Be sure to seek legal and financial advice before getting involved in a syndicate. The returns may seem to be slightly higher than with property trusts, but consider what would happen in a sudden period of upheaval, such as losing your job, or a family crisis or relocation to another country? Can you get out of it if you have to? How much do you stand to lose if you have to bail out early? Again, other people have control here, not you. This may suit some people, but, personally, I like a more hands-on approach!

Direct property investment. Direct property has been a form of investment for centuries. The word 'landlord' features in the Bible! I have chosen direct property investment as the main investment vehicle for myself and for my investment network – so in later chapters I will cover property and related general investment strategies in more detail. What follows here is a broad outline of direct property investment.

Many of you have already experienced some of the financial implications of buying a property when you bought your own home. It is a little different when buying an investment property. The basics are the same whichever form of property you choose to invest in – commercial, industrial or residential.

There are set up costs, but many of these can be partially or totally deducted against the named owner or owners' taxable incomes and can even drop investors into a lower tax bracket. (This tax reduction is not a reason to invest in anything, unless it can also generate some capital growth and income.) There is often a deposit to be found (although this is not always the case, as you will see in Chapter 6).

There is a list of initial and ongoing expenses, many of which can be claimed against income as tax deductions. These deductions could include the interest component of any loan you take out to buy a property for investment purposes, the legal fees, the stamp duty, the fees for necessary repair costs, depreciation of building and its fittings and a few other expenses too!

There is income generated by the property in the form of rent. There is the option of paying a property manager to manage your property and collect your rent for you. (The property manager's fees are also tax-deductible.)

Finding the right property. Many people think of property investment as risky and expensive. Yes, there are some risks, as there are with all equity investments, but risk can be managed and minimised. There is the risk that a property, if badly chosen in the first place, will go untenanted for more than a couple of weeks in one year, thus losing you income. Another risk, if the property has not been thoroughly researched and inspected, is that it might cost you so much money to make it liveable for tenants and to maintain it in that condition, that it will take many years before you show a clear profit on it. These problems are avoidable if the property is bought with tenanting in mind – and if you buy with your head and not your heart!

The other thing to bear in mind is – how much can you afford? There is no real benefit in buying a property that you struggle to make the loan repayments on if four or five weeks with no tenant and no rent means you have to sell it. Do your sums and work out what level of financial input you are comfortable with. Property, like any equity investment needs to be kept for the long term, 10 years or more, for it to generate optimum growth and returns.

Get information through real estate agents and the Real Estate Institute of whichever state you plan to buy in about rental returns for the areas which interest you. Another tip is to buy local – in the same city or town that you live in – and only buy after a personal assessment, rather than buying sight-unseen in another State. Before you laugh at the possibility of doing something so silly, many people have done this and had their fingers burned very badly. Chapter 4 includes some property scams that made millions for the vendors – at the expense of the buyers.

Make sure your solicitor checks the sales contract. Make sure you chose an independent pest and building inspector. If the seller, or vendor, recommends inspectors to you, politely thank them and make your own arrangements. If the vendor claims a certain amount of rent will be realised, visit a few local real estate agents and check out the rental returns on similar properties. At REIN, this is an important part of what we do.

In a nutshell, residential property, whilst the most common vehicle for private investors, has a slightly lower average rate of return (rents against expenses) than commercial property. On average, commercial property can charge slightly higher rents per purchase dollar, but run the risk of being hit by a recession in the economy. Residential property, while its capital growth may be slowed, stalled or even go backwards in a recession, can still be reasonably sure of tenants, even if the rents have to drop a little or stay at their current level for longer than you would like. People still need somewhere to live, even when businesses are going bust. Industrial property also has a slightly higher rate of returns than residential through higher rent levels, but, again, is more at risk of going untenanted through a downturn in the economy and the subsequent repercussions on industry. The other factor is the initial start up costs and the size of the loan needed for commercial and industrial property purchases. They may be out of the reach of first-time property investors, unless they join a syndicate.

Growth and returns. The capital growth of your property investment depends on the property itself – its location, condition, size and features. It also depends on the overall market. As already mentioned, the market is cyclic, so property has to be a long-term proposition in order to ride out the lows that will occur.

Research as to location is vital. On average, growth in cities and inner city suburbs has given higher returns than growth in suburbs an hour's drive away from the city centre. Growth in properties that are waterfront, close to water, or have water views is also, on average, higher than in those that are landlocked. Facilities surrounding the property play their part too. Restaurants nearby, parks, shopping centres and easy access to public transport are features that will encourage both tenancy and capital growth.

Research through the Real Estate Institute of your State and local real estate agents will give you an indication of how the market has behaved in the areas you are looking at. Keep an eye on the local papers too. They often have the prices of properties realised at auctions. Look around and compare sales prices, conditions and locations.

The average figure for yearly growth is currently between 6 and 9 per cent, but a poor building in a sleazy inner city district, or a house far from the city centre or out in the bush somewhere will realise less. This is of course unless the sleazy inner city district gets tarted up and becomes the next Paddington, or the country town that you bought your property in becomes the next Byron Bay. The chances of this are higher than winning millions in the lottery, but I would still be very hesitant to take such a gamble.

As the property increases in value, all profits, after expenses have been covered and inflation is taken into account, are subject to capital gains tax when you sell the property. Currently, all equity assets bought after the end of 1999 and held for over a year can be subject to a choice of inflation adjustment or paying capital gains tax on only 50 per cent of the gain. Work it out. If you hold the property for 15 years and then sell, you might actually be better off asking for an inflation adjustment rather than the 50 per cent deal. This is particularly true in times of higher inflation rates. Talk to your accountant before you sell and realise the capital gain.

C H A P T E R   6

WHY I PUT MY MONEY ON PROPERTY

f I was given a dollar for every time I have been asked the question 'What gives the best return, shares or property?' I would be at least a few thousand dollars richer. The answer is that shares perform better than property over the long term. If shares outperform property, why then would I keep using property investment as my vehicle on the path to wealth? It's simple really. I can borrow up to 100 per cent of what I need from the bank to buy property, using my existing equity. When it comes to shares, banks will rarely give you more than about 60 per cent. They prefer the lower risk, lower volatility and greater security of bricks and mortar.

If I have $300,000 equity in my own home I can borrow $300,000 for an investment property. I can only borrow about $180,000 if I choose to buy shares. This increases my ability to generate returns from my investments because the more I am able to invest, the greater the leverage and the better the outcome.

According to the Real Estate Institute of Australia, the median yearly capital growth on residential investment properties was 7.8 per cent over the last 20 years. I have been using the figure of 6 per cent throughout this book. This gives me the peace of mind that even at lower than average growth, my investment system will still work.

Studies have also demonstrated that capital growth levels increase as

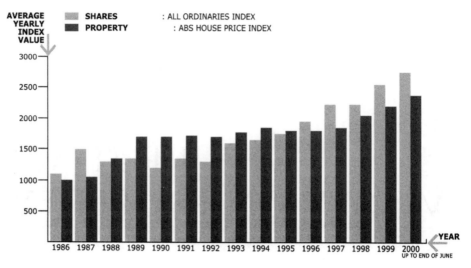

AVERAGE
YEARLY
INDEX
VALUE

SHARES : ALL ORDINARIES INDEX
PROPERTY : ABS HOUSE PRICE INDEX

YEAR

1986 1987 1988 1989 1990 1991 1992 1993 1994 1995 1996 1997 1998 1999 2000
UP TO END OF JUNE

SOURCE: COLONIAL FIRST STATE, AUSTRALIA BUREAU OF STATISTICS & AUSTRALIAN STOCK EXCHANGE

Performance of shares and property, 1986 to 2000

you get closer to the CBD, where they are at their highest. One such study, completed by the Australian Property Information Centre over 25 years, from 1967 to 1992, found that capital growth was significantly higher in suburbs closest to the CBD and tailed off considerably as they headed out into suburbia. This strengthens my decision to buy in or around the CBD.

How the comparisons add up. An average 6 per cent capital growth on a $300,000 property over 15 years gives me around $750,000 as a gross result. On $180,000 worth of shares at an average 6 per cent, I will end up with around $450,000. In the meantime, my residential property has been paying for itself over the 15 years with rental returns and tax minimisations that shares cannot equal. I will be able to claim tax deductions over the 15 years on property that tax deductions on shares will not be able to give me.

The actual annual gross return for shares from 1980 to 2000, according to the Australian Stock Exchange, was 13.2 per cent (this included returns through dividend payments as well as capital growth). The annual gross return for residential investment property over the same period based on the results from six major capital cities in Australia was 15.6 per cent (including rent returns as well as capital growth), according to the Real Estate Institute of Australia.

If we look at the tax situation with shares, the interest on the original loan and any brokerage fees can be claimed against tax. Some or all of the tax already paid by companies on their shares before you buy them can be claimed back through the dividend imputation scheme (to avoid a blatantly unfair double taxing on shares).

"Readily may thou borrow to pay the brickmaker and the builder"
George S Clason

On a residential property, not only can you claim the interest on the loan, but also any management fees, depreciation, certain insurances, materials and fees for maintenance, rates and so on. Share dividends are financially the equivalent of rental returns, but, unless you can put the same amount of investment capital into your shares in the first place, these dividends will not equal rent.

There is also the risk that if I choose to buy shares, by the time I want to retire, settle my loan and invest the profit, it might be a really bad time to sell shares. When they rise, they can rise like a skyrocket. When they fall, the falls can be spectacular too!

All in all, I can borrow more, meaning less cost and greater leverage to me, if I buy property. It is more tax effective in the long run and gives me excellent returns with less volatility and more peace of mind. This is why I keep buying residential investment properties to secure my financial future.

Russell and Theresa

Russell and Theresa, both in their mid-thirties, came to one of my seminars a few years ago. They were curious as to why I worked with property as my investment vehicle and not shares, as they had been told that shares were top performers and property would not give them the returns that shares could. We met later and I went through the figures for them to demonstrate my reasons more clearly.

They had $320,000 equity in their own home, which was worth $480,000 at that time. If they had gone to a bank or lending institution with this equity and had taken out a loan to buy shares, they might have got a loan of $192,000. If we work out their figures over 25 years and assume an average interest rate of 8 per cent for the first few years, let's track their investment potential with shares.

With Shares. They use the loan to purchase $190,000 worth of shares through a broker. They can claim brokerage fees and the interest on this loan against tax. They can also get some tax refunds on the franked part of their shares (see previous section on shares in Chapter 5). They will be receiving dividends from their shares, which will help to pay the interest on the loan. The tax refunds and dividends will probably cover most of their interest payments, so their investment will be paid for in this way. Twenty-five years down the track, they sell their portfolio, now worth $800,000 dollars. After capital gains tax and repayment of the original loan, they are left with around $490,000. If they then invest this at 6 per cent average yearly returns, it will give them a gross return of around $565 a week.

With property. What happens if they choose property in the first place? They will be able to borrow $320,000. They buy a property worth $300,000 in the CBD and are able to rent it for $320 a week. They have an average of 50 weeks rental a year coming in. There will be tax returns on their interest payments, the depreciation and other costs associated with investment property. Including the rent coming in, the property actually starts off costing them $40 a week, which is reduced to nothing after three or four years and then goes into profit after that, creating new opportunities for investment.

The value of the property after 25 years is around $1,200,000. After they sell and pay out the loan, costs and capital gains tax, they are left with around $680,000. If this is invested to give an average yearly return of 6 per cent, they will receive a gross return of around $785 a week.

So, for no extra cost to the investors, they will be $220 a week better off if they choose property against shares. Russell and Theresa chose property. They now own their second property and are looking at buying a third property in the next few months. They will have reached their goal of wealth in retirement before they reach 60.

Using an effective system.

Through my work with REIN, I have learned much about property investment and have developed a system by which investors can generate financial independence. One of the principles of the system, investing as a group of 30 to 40 under the same organisation and gaining leverage by sheer weight of numbers, cannot be used by the individual, but the majority of the system's underlying structure is suitable for use by the sole investor.

The first principle that is illustrated by my system is that of making an informed decision. Without information, we are guessing. The second principle is to minimise risk wherever possible. If every decision you make is an informed decision, you are contributing heavily to the process of risk minimisation. These principles can be applied to any investment option. If you are looking at share investment, it would make sense to know what the companies you are targeting have achieved and what the forecasts are for their future performance. It is wise to find out if they are currently considering mergers with other companies or are likely to be taken over – this will affect their share value. If you are looking at managed funds – who is giving the best overall performance and what level of risk would suit you best? This is called doing your homework!

With residential property investment, the chosen vehicle of myself and my clients, our first assignment is to be fully informed by uncovering the sort of home the tenant we want to attract is looking for – and creating less risk of vacancy or low rental returns.

Know your tenant!

The process of buying a residential property for investment begins with the tenant. When I say to investors that we buy a tenant first, then we pay for the property, I often get blank looks! All it means is that we select a property that we know from past and current experience will attract the sort of tenant that we want. In order to do this successfully, we have to know our tenant's desires and preferences. Knowing that, if the property matches these preferences, we can 'buy safe' with the knowledge that the property will have no problems in finding and keeping a tenant from the start.

One of the problems many residential property investors face because of their age and their values, is that they tend to buy properties they believe would make their tenants happy. However, their understanding of

"Let's pick number seven — I reckon he's ideal!"

what makes a tenant happy is based on what they themselves would be happy with. They have little concept of what a 25 year old wants today, so they buy an unsuitable property and wonder what went wrong.

Our ideal tenants are probably from the so-called 'Generation X' (early 20s to mid 30s). They are single or childless couples. They are working in demanding, well-paid careers and are still young. Home has taken on a new meaning and a new function for them. It is no longer the three-bedroom house in a nice, quiet street. A back garden for the kids, a large kitchen with breakfast bar, a separate dining room, family room, wall to wall carpet and the two-car garage are not needed for a single professional or a couple with no children, a demanding career and no time to mow the lawn.

They want their home to be streamlined, labour-saving and to reflect their new lifestyle. Some of the units and apartments in Sydney and Melbourne's CBDs have kitchens too small to swing a cat in, if they have the time or inclination to have a cat! Some do not even have conventional ovens, just a microwave, a dishwasher, a waste disposal unit and a freezer full of ready-cooked gourmet meals!

At the beginning of the book I wrote about the changing nature of our country's population. Then we looked at the demographic impact on pensions and the welfare system. We now need to study the impact of the changes on the property markets. The 'Australian dream' of owning your own home in the suburbs on a quarter acre block with a Hills Hoist and a Victa two-stroke is losing its grip on the minds of younger generations. 'Gen X' and the next generation to follow, the 'Dot.Coms', (from the 'com' of email addresses) are no longer sure whether they want to own a house anymore. Lifestyle is important to them. Convenience, style, comfort and ease of living make up a large part of that lifestyle

Many 20-something and 30-something professionals are realising they cannot afford the sort of place they actually want to live in and so they choose to rent. They are choosing lifestyle over home ownership. Let's imagine these Gen X's and Dot.Coms can afford $450 a week, as either rent or mortgage payment. They are faced with a choice between buying an old unit or a small house out west for around $350,000 or renting something new in the style they want to live in, in the place they want to live.

Charlie's story. Charlie is in his mid 20s and is renting one of my investment properties in Pyrmont, in Sydney's inner city, with stunning views of Darling Harbour and the city. He works in the CBD and can walk to work each day. It is a one-bedroom unit and currently rents for $450 a week. Charlie's dad came with him to view the place before Charlie signed the lease – and did his best to dissuade Charlie from taking it. His dad could not understand why he would pay rent when he could buy a place. Charlie was adamant in his choice. Even if he did use the rent to pay a mortgage he could not afford more than around $320,000. What would that buy him? A three-bedroom house in the outer-western suburbs of Sydney's sprawl?

Charlie wanted to live in the City. He chose to rent a place to suit his lifestyle. He did not want to live where he could afford to buy. His dad cannot understand his son's way of thinking. They agreed to differ!

People like Charlie have a preference for living within 5-10 km of Sydney's CBD because most of them work there or on the Lower North Shore. They want to live close to public transport, so they do not have to drive a car to work, nor do they have to walk far. They want to be close to restaurants and cafes, to shopping centres, to the water and parks. They don't want gardens, they want views.

The new Manhattan. Developers are not slow to act on these changes in demand. The new developments going up around the CBDs of Sydney, Melbourne, Adelaide, Perth and Brisbane has led to the coining of a new term, 'Manhattanisation'! The most densely populated area of Sydney is Kings Cross at 33,000 people per square kilometre. It isn't far behind New York City's Manhattan Island at 58,000 people per square kilometre.

The City of Sydney is the fastest growing municipality in Australia, according to the tenth annual population study released by KPMG in 1999. In 1998 there was an increase of 25.5 per cent in its population. In 1997 the population growth was 15 per cent.

In 1999, when Mirvac released 82 apartments for sale in a development in Pyrmont in Sydney, they sold 81 in ONE DAY! Similar trends have been noted in Melbourne. In Port Melbourne in the same year it took just 10 days to sell 200 apartments in a 320-apartment block. Some of these sales were being made to the 'baby boomers' who no longer have children at home and who want a change in their lifestyle. Investors bought the other apartments, looking for high rental returns from Generation X. Almost half of Sydney's city residents are aged between 22 and 36. Whilst these Gen X's make up 23 per cent of the general population, they make up 42 per cent of the population of Sydney City. If you are an intelligent investor, you will be looking to buy what they want.★

★(Bernard Salt – 'The Big Shift' KPMG tenth annual population growth report – 1999)

Dream over. The demise of the so-called 'Australian Dream' means some rethinking for those of us who have bought larger houses out in the suburbs. If the next two or three generations are not interested in living in the outer suburbs of Sydney, who will buy our houses when we want to sell and buy something smaller? Many people plan to do this, particularly people who have not put any money away in investments for when they cease to get an income from employment. The idea behind their thinking is that they will be able to make a large profit by downsizing their home and then can invest the profit to generate enough income return to live on.

As we know, there are two flaws to this way of thinking. One is that time is needed for investments to be of use to us. Leaving it that late in life is leaving it too late. The other flaw is that there is no guarantee that a house in the outer suburbs will appreciate in value in the same way as a house or unit in the inner suburbs and the inner city.

What the new generations want and why

I am no longer interested in buying investment properties that are in need of repair, that can only be let for a low rent and will need a high level of maintenance because of the property's age and initial condition. I want tenants of a certain earning capacity to make sure I get the level of rent I want and to make sure I get it consistently. I want low maintenance and a property I can claim maximum depreciation on to offset my expenses. (I will explain all of the tax and finance structures and benefits in detail in the next chapter.)

I want the property in a place the tenant wants to live in. In other words, in Sydney I want a new unit in an apartment block in the CBD or within 10 kilometres radius of Centrepoint Tower. It must be less than 500 metres away from a train station or public transport system suitable for commuters. My tenants don't want to drive to work. There is too much traffic and nowhere to park. My tenants don't want to walk far, there's not enough time in their busy schedules. My tenants want to be near large shopping centres for variety, choice and convenience of under-one-roof shopping. My tenants need cafes, restaurants and takeaway outlets for when they are too tired or too late to cook. My tenants wants to be near cinemas, bars and clubs. A large park or water would be nice too!

My tenants want security, so an apartment block needs to have security cameras and on-site security night and day. My tenants want the convenience of a gym and a swimming pool, so there are no journeys to the gym and no expensive gym memberships to pay out. They want secure parking and allocated car spaces for the BMW, off-roader or sports coupé. And don't forget the built-in dishwasher, microwave and dryer!

Where do I find all this? I look at all the proposed developments going up within a 10 kilometre radius of the CBD that also fit the criteria of being less than half a kilometre to public transport and close to a large shopping centre. I check the credentials and reputation of the developer and start looking at the plans for the developments to see if they will answer the needs of my, as yet, imaginary tenant. Only then do I start asking about prices, because a bargain price on an apartment is no good to me if I can't get a tenant to rent it. I normally buy 'off the plan' once I have checked out the developer's credentials. This gives me a discounted price and generally means that by the time I have to settle on the property, its value has already risen, often by tens of thousands of dollars! Instant equity!

"I'll take it!"

Opportunity Knocks!

This illustrates another principle of effective investment. When opportunity knocks at your door, let it in.

In buying an investment property that doesn't exist in concrete terms yet, I can make money immediately. This is because of being first in and aiming to buy 'off the plan', before the building has even been built. I can save tens and perhaps even hundreds of thousands of dollars, because I buy when there are few other buyers around. By the time it is up and ready for settlement, the value has often increased by as much as $50,000 or more!

Not many people see a hole in the ground as a prime opportunity for investment. It takes imagination and courage. Previous experience and research to base my decision on helps enormously. When you have information, the fear of doing something different is lessened and the risk is minimised.

Imagine buying shares in a new company. It has no track record, no reputation and no previous history. The first thing you need to do is your homework. Compare it to similar companies in similar locations to get an idea of how it might perform. Find out who is running it and what they have achieved before they started this company. Consider the potential of their product or service and identify the major backers of the company and their experience and reputations. In this way you are able to min- imise considerably the risk of investing in the unknown.

You can then go on to buy into the company and take advantage of buying very low priced shares that, if you have succeeded in your research, will increase in value considerably over time. The important part of this strategy is getting the information and doing the research before you put your hand in your pocket. Talking to someone who has already done this is necessary. Talking to experts, such as reputable stock brokers or property investment advisors, reading the appropriate books and peri- odicals or visiting the relevant web sites are all recommended too. Make sure your information is from a reputable source, is up to date and is appropriate to the Australian markets.

The point here is that timing your investment purchases can make a difference to your overall returns. If you are willing to open your mind to opportunity, it usually comes knocking. You also need to be able to recognise it when it does knock and have the courage to invite it in!

C H A P T E R   7

HOW TO GET HOLD OF OTHER PEOPLE'S MONEY!

A t this stage, the best laid plans of mice, men and investors will need financing. Many people fear getting into debt, particularly when we're talking here of hundreds of thousands of dollars. Having read this far, I am going to assume that, in theory at least, you are open to the opportunities that borrowing will give you – and you are committed to working towards the financially independent future that awaits you at the end of your wealth plan.

My advice here is to use trained brokers or bankers who are experienced in setting up loans for investors. Ask them about their track record in securing loans for investment.

The realisation of your plans will need help from a lending institution. How do you know that the lending body will shake your hand and not show you the door? Step into the shoes of a loans officer at your average bank. What is important to them? SECURITY. You will need to convince them that they will get their money back plus the interest. They need to feel confident that you can pay how much you say you will, when you say you will. They need to have some form of a guarantee that they can recover the amount of the loan should you become incapacitated or die. They need to be able to trust that you will not, on receipt of the money, run off to South America on a false passport and disappear!

If you already own your own home, even if you have not paid it all off, you are off to a flying start. You have already proved to the bank or lending body that you have the ability to pay off a loan. You have a property behind you, and equity in that property that can act as a guarantee. It also tells the bank that you are a stable member of the community. It takes time to sell a house, so that sudden and unexpected trip to South America looks far less likely to the loans officer.

(By the way, just because you have your existing mortgage with one particular bank does not mean you have to stay with that bank. Shop around for an investment loan and get information on several loan packages. Find out how much it would cost in bank charges, how convenient it is and what facilities it can offer. You can even try to haggle over the interest rates if you find a loan package you like, but it has a higher rate than the rate at the bank next door.)

The bank will want to know your pedigree, so be prepared to answer a variety of questions! They will want to know your residency status, your employment and income details and those of your spouse or partner, if you have one. They'll want to know about any children you have, any dependents from previous relationships or marriages that have a call on your income. They'll want to know how long you have lived in your current home and even your previous home. They'll also check your credit rating and your credit history. They will ask for value of your assets, investment assets, cars, boats, furniture, whitegoods, home entertainment units, jewellery and other articles. (Banks have a different definition of assets than financially intelligent investors do! Funny, that!)

For those of you who are self-employed and who may be used to making the most of their expenses and the least of their incomes for tax purposes, you will need to reverse this approach. The name of the game here is income maximisation and you will be asked to show income records for several years before they will consider you a suitable risk for a loan. You may have to enlist the aid of your accountant for this, but stick to reality. There is no point in convincing the bank that you can pay off a loan if the real story is different and it means using all your available income to do so.

I have known people who were earning over $100,000 a year and only declaring $15,000. This may have reduced their tax bills, but is no help when it comes to investing. I would rather declare all my income and then swap tax for investment in assets, through tax deductions. In my experience, paying less tax by declaring less income may reduce your tax bill, but means you cannot borrow to invest and so you cannot secure a wealthy future.

So far so good! You have convinced the lending body that you are not bankrupt, that you have both the intention and the ability to pay back a loan and that you are not an unemployed mime artist with five kids and a list of previous addresses longer than the 'phone book! The next step for the lending body is to calculate what is known as the Loan to Value Ratio (LVR).

Ray and Cathy. Ray and Cathy are both in their late 30s. They have one child and are paying off their home in an inner-west suburb of Sydney. Ray works full-time as a training manager for a large communications company. He's been there for the last seven years and is currently on an income of $56,000 a year. Cathy works part-time as a nurse, doing three shifts a week. She's been at the hospital where she is employed for three years now. When they bought their family home 12 years ago they were both working full-time and it was worth $165,000. They had saved up their deposit of $18,000 before approaching the bank to get their home loan.

The bank assessed them as stable, secure wage earners with a good credit rating and an acceptable LVR. They needed to borrow $147,000. The value of the house was $165,000. The LVR was worked out by dividing the loan value by the house value, multiplied by 100.

$$\frac{\$\ 147,000}{\$\ 165,000} \quad \text{x } 100 \ = \ 89.09 \text{ per cent}$$

They were both earning reasonable full-time wages making their joint income look very healthy, so the bank was happy with this LVR and gave them their loan.

Now, 12 years down the track, they have decided to buy a residential investment property and have approached the bank for a loan. They still owe around $28,000 on their current house. After assessing their income and all the other details, the bank now works out their new LVR. This takes into account the fact that they have increased equity in a house now worth around $320,000. They want to borrow $350,000 for a new $330,000 town house also in the inner-west and have no deposit. The bank works out the total loan.

$ 28,000 + (existing amount owed on own house)
$ 350,000 (new loan for investment property)
$ 378,000

The bank now works out the value of total properties which is

$ 320,000 + (value of own home)
$ 330,000 (value of investment property)
$ 650,000

The LVR is then calculated as before

$$\frac{\$\ 378,000}{\$\ 650,000} \times 100 = \textbf{58.15 per cent}$$

Looking at this and then looking at the income and outgoings of Ray and Cathy's finances, the bank gave approval to Ray and Cathy for their investment loan.

Two years later they wanted to buy another investment property. At this stage they had paid off the family home. This was another investment property in the next suburb to their original investment property. They needed a loan of $380,000 for this one. The cost of the actual property was $360,000.

They went back to the bank and the bank did the calculations. The total loan value would be

$ 350,000 + (loan on investment property #1)
$ 380,000 (new loan for investment property #2)
$ 730,000

The bank now works out the value of total properties which is

$ 320,000 + (value of own home)
$ 330,000 + (value of investment property #1)
$ 360,000 (value of investment property #2)
$ 1,010,000

The LVR is then calculated as before

$$\frac{\$\ 730{,}000}{\$\ 1{,}010{,}000} \times 100 = \textbf{72.28 per cent}$$

The bank now needs to calculate whether they have the means and ability to pay off this total loan package. This ability to 'service' the loan is called the Debt Service Ratio (DSR). This is calculated to reassure the bank that Ray and Cathy will be able to pay the bank back and will depend on their income, their current debts and loan repayments – and the rents from the investment properties. 'DSR' is known by many names and lending bodies may have different formulas for working it out, but the aim remains the same – can they afford it? This calculation is worked out by the bank for every loan, after they have worked out the LVR.

In this example, and this is a very common method, the total loan repayments are divided by Ray and Cathy's eligible income. This is calculated by using 30 per cent of total wages and 80 per cent of the rents coming in before tax. It does not take into account tax rebates or irregular earnings such as sporadic overtime. Ray and Cathy earn a total gross combined salary of $82,000. The total rents on both properties will be $680 a week.

In Ray and Cathy's case, paying interest of 7.2 per cent, fixed for five years on both their investment property loans, the figures would be:

Loan payments
Repayments per year on $730,000 total loan at 7.2% = **$ 52,560**

Eligible income
30% of total salaries of $82,000   = $ 24,600 +
80% of total rents from properties of $35,360   = $ 28,288
                                                                                      $ 52,888

DSR   =   **99.38%**

The DSR is a percentage calculation. In this case $52,560 is 99.38 per cent of $52,888. Most banks are happy to give the go ahead on loans as long as the DSR is 100 per cent or less (in other words, the loan repayments are equal to, or less than eligible income). So Ray and Cathy have just made it, in the eyes of the bank.

How though, does it really work out for them? Firstly, what will be the tax benefits to them and how much will this put in their pockets? Since Ray is the main salary earner, with his gross income of $56,000 a

year from his employment, it was decided to put the investment properties in his name. With rents of $35,360, this takes his total income for the
year to $91,360. Now let's take into account the deductions he can make.

Ray's gross income	=	**$ 91,360**
Rental deductions		
Interest	=	$ 52,560 +
Property expenses (approx 25% of rent)	=	$ 8,840 +
Depreciation on buildings	=	$ 6,800 +
Depreciation on fittings	=	$ 9,180 +
Borrowing costs	=	$ 1,700 +
		$ 79,080
		$ 91,360 –
		$ 79,080
Ray's new gross income	=	**$ 12,280**

Now let's look again at the yearly costs for Ray and Cathy, now we
have taken the new tax situation into account.

Expenses		
Ray's tax on $12,280	=	$ 1,068 +
Cathy's tax on $26,000	=	$ 4,180 +
Rental expenses	=	$ 8,840 +
Loan repayment (interest only)	=	$ 52,560 +
Living expenses	=	$ 32,000 +
Total expenditure for the year		**$ 98,648**
Income		
Ray's gross salary	=	$ 56,000 +
Cathy's gross salary	=	$ 26,000 +
Rental income	=	$ 35,360 +
Total income for the year		**$ 117,360**

When they deduct the expenses from the incomes they are in fact
working with **a surplus of $18,712!** This could be used for rainy day
money – a buffer against vacant tenancies or unforeseen expenses. Or
they could invest some or all of it in shares or managed funds, or wait for

two or three more years and buy another investment property, but actually borrow less, because they have a ready-made deposit.

In 20 years time, when they are both ready to retire, they will be able to sell the properties and use the profits to invest in an income generating investment such as managed funds.

What will these properties add to the income they will have from their superannuation? The value of these properties will be around $1,700,000 (a conservative estimate). The capital gains tax and sales costs will come to around $280,000. The loan still stands at $730,000. Once they have paid out the loan and covered the costs, they are looking at a net profit of $690,000. If they invest this at a 6 per cent average yearly return, they will generate a gross yearly income, on top of their super, of $41,400.

The interest-only loan

Throughout this book the investors mentioned have used an interest-only loan. At this point it is worth going over why this type of loan is a common choice of the financially intelligent investor.

It increases your leverage. With an interest-only loan, you have the option and the capacity to buy more than one investment property. As you know, this gives you greater profits on retirement, which is what this is all about. The less time you have on your side, the more effective multiple properties are. If one property will make you a profit of $180,000, three similar properties, bought within one or two years of each other, will make you a profit of $500,000. At 6 per cent average yearly return, that is the difference between an extra $10,800 a year retirement income on top of your super and an extra $30,000 a year income. Which would you rather have?

If you went the same way as when you bought your family home and took out a principal and interest loan, it would cost the average investor too much to buy and hold more than one property every 10 or so years.

It gives you greater control of your finances. Interest-only loans can be fixed at a certain rate for periods of, commonly, up to five years. After this the bank expects you to pay out the loan or refinance for another fixed period. Knowing exactly how much you will need to pay each week helps you to budget and reduces the worry and stress of rising interest rates for the fixed period.

ARTCHA '02

"... then you take the other dollar and step into a time machine."

Inflation is on your side. Inflation means the amount of principal you borrow will be worth comparatively less when you do finally pay it back. Working on an average yearly inflation of 4 per cent, if you borrow $500,000 today and pay it back in 16 years, you are still paying back $500,000, but it will only buy $270,000 worth of anything in 16 years. In 16 years the dollar today will only buy about 54 cents worth of goods.

Imagine you have $2 in your pocket. You buy a kilo of carrots for $1 at the local fruit market. Then you take the other dollar and step into a time machine (I did say "Imagine"!) and step out at exactly the same fruit market 16 years later and go to buy some more carrots. You will only be able to buy half a kilo, because they are now $2 per kilo. Of course the wages of the workers in 16 years will have doubled too. So that dollar you borrowed 16 years ago and are paying back now is costing you half as much than if you had paid it back soon after borrowing it.

HOW MUCH INVESTMENT IS ENOUGH?

A t the beginning of the book I outlined a definition of wealth according to Buckminster Fuller. To save you losing your place, here it is again, **"I am wealthy when I have an income stream that will generate enough money to live the lifestyle I desire before I get out of bed in the morning."** In order to plan your investment strategy successfully, you now need to put a figure to this concept of wealth to ensure that you have a large enough investment portfolio to generate the level of wealth you need. Every person I talk to has a different idea of what wealth means to them.

When a person who is interested in residential property investment meets with me, one of the first things we will do is discuss what it means to them to retire with financial independence and what level of comfort they want in their retirement. I then work with them on creating what I call a **'compelling future'.** All we do is estimate how much money they are going to need on retirement. Setting a clear and detailed goal is the first stage in any successful investment plan – as you know. I ask them to imagine their lives after retirement, what they will want to do, how much it will cost to live the way they want – and then we work backwards from there to find out the best way of achieving this goal.

Imagine that this person is you. How do we begin? First I need to find out some information on where you are up to at this stage in your life. Do you own your own home? How much is it currently worth and how much, if anything, do you still owe on it? With this information I can work out what level of equity you already have. It may be that you have never considered the idea of the equity in your home. For me, that's like having a huge pile of dollars sitting in your front room doing absolutely nothing, because you haven't noticed it!

"I know investing is a great idea, but where would we find the money?"

Next, I'll ask you to consider when you intend to retire, so that we know how long we've got to work with. Then I'll ask you to consider how you want to live your life in retirement. I find this is easily done and easy to put a figure on if we take it in three stages. The first step is to write down the '*must* haves' of your life in retirement. Assuming that you will have paid off your house then, you will still need to cover things like rates, electricity, telephone, insurance of home and contents and car, maintenance of your home, the running of one or two cars, the money to replace one or both of those cars every few years, health fund fees, clothing and shoes, replacement of household items and, of course, food. Not only will I ask you to list your '*must* haves', but also to put a current value on each of them.

The second step is to consider the 'should haves'. These items are the things in life that change your standard of living from having absolute necessities only, to a more enjoyable standard of living. From 'no frills' to 'some frills', if you like!

Items such as holidays in Australia, eating out, going to the dog track, buying gifts for loved ones, newspapers, books and magazines and other non-necessities.

The third step is to list the 'could haves'. These might be holidays overseas, establishing a wine cellar, club memberships and fees and other items that establish a 'more frills' lifestyle. Your 'should haves' and 'could haves' lists will be different to those of other people. Your 'must haves' list will probably be quite similar. Once you have calculated the costs of these lists and added them all together, you will have an idea of how much you will need as a yearly income to live the life you choose, rather than the life you are stuck with.

Working out the figures

Let's imagine I'm working this out for a couple living in north-west Sydney who are contemplating their lives after retirement. Their two children will have left home and both will be working. The couple will still be members of different clubs and will have one car, which they will trade in and upgrade every five or six years. They will have paid off their house completely. They will be able to have a couple of holidays a year, one being an overseas trip. They will be able to go out for dinner once or twice a week and go to the cinema or theatre at least once a fortnight.

We start by building up the three lists. The 'must haves' list, then the 'should haves' list, and finally the 'could haves' list and cost them to reflect 15 years inflation.

N.B. The cost of each item in the lists has been increased to allow for inflation at an approximate rate of 3 per cent over a 15-year period. In the last six years the rise in the annual cost of living has been averaged out as less than 3 per cent per annum.

List 1 'must haves'

per year

A roof over our heads

Maintenance	$ 4,000
Rates/water rates	$ 2,150
Electricity	$ 1,100
Telephone	$ 1,200
Insurance	$ 1,500

Transport (per car, allowing for savings to buy a
new car every 5-6 years, service, repairs, petrol etc.) $ 10,200

Health	$ 2,800
Food, clothes etc	$ 11,700
Total 'must haves'	**$ 34,650**

List 2 'should haves'

per year

Holidays in Australia	$ 6,000
Eating out once or twice a week	$ 6,000
Movies once or twice a fortnight	$ 1,800
Gifts	$ 1,500
Papers/Periodicals/Books	$ 1,125
Total 'should haves'	**$ 16,425**
Add 'must haves'	+ $ 34,650
Total 'must haves' + 'should haves'	= **$ 51,075**

List 3 'could haves'

per year

Holidays overseas	$ 11,250
Beer/wine	$ 2,250
Club, club fees	$ 2,250
Total 'could haves'	**$ 15,750**
Add 'must haves' and 'should haves'	+ $ 51,075
Total 'must haves, should haves, could haves'	= **$ 66,825**

The example above gives us a net total of $66,825 that the couple from north-west Sydney needs each year to live their retirement in the way they want. If we allow that their super is rolled over into a government-approved annuity or pension and therefore $18,000 of their income will be tax-free, we still need to allow for tax on the rest of their income.

If we reduce the $66,825 that they need by the $18,000 from their super, they still have to find $48,825 net (after tax). To end up with $48,825 net, they need to generate $60,000 gross (before tax). The amount they need to generate to afford the 'could haves' as well as the 'must haves' and 'should haves' is therefore:

$18,000 + $60,000 = $78,000 per year

The nest egg

The next step is to work out what sort of investment value, or nest egg, the couple will need to generate such a yearly income, assuming a conservative 6 per cent per annum appreciation of their investments has been achieved by the time they wish to retire.

I use a very simple formula that anyone with a calculator can follow – *multiply the net yearly income needed by a factor of 16.5.*

$78,000 x 16.5 = $1,287,000 (the amount of the nest egg)

The $1,287,000 nest egg earning 6 per cent will yield just under $78,000 gross each year.

How are we going to create such a large nest egg? Most people I have worked with on their compelling futures have initially looked horrified at such figures.

Once we get through the next stage, they look a lot happier!

What happens with no plan of action?

In the example above, our couple own a home in West Pennant Hills which has a current market value of $450,000. They still owe $100,000 to the bank. He is aged 40 and working full time. She is aged 37 and is currently working in the family home, caring for the family, including their two children who are aged 8 and 11. He currently has $30,000 in his superannuation fund. They have $5,000 sitting in a bank account – their 'emergency money'.

This couple have not yet considered a plan for creating financial independence in retirement. As yet they have no goal and no understanding of how they will exist once his income ceases. What will happen?

They are looking forward to paying the house off in approximately 12 years. Then they want to use the extra dollars available to improve their lifestyle. A holiday overseas, a new car, eating out more, new furniture. After all, the kids will be grown up and mum and dad are looking forward to having extra time and extra money to enjoy life to the full. Three years after paying off the house he will retire. Fifteen years down the track the house will be worth around $900,000 and his super fund will be worth about $300,000. They'll be worth more than a million! He wants to retire at 55, to enjoy this 'wealth' and live in comfort.

When he does retire, the 'wealth' he has assumed he had isn't available to him. His super will generate about $18,000 a year, tax-free, if rolled over into an approved pension or annuity. His home may be worth hundreds of thousands, but, unless they choose to sell and move to a much smaller place, it gives them nothing but more expenditure. It certainly doesn't earn them anything. At $18,000 per annum, they can't even afford the 'must haves' list.

What if they do sell their treasured family home? Let's imagine they get $900,000 for it. They will need to find somewhere else to live. They want to stay in Sydney because the kids and their other family and friends are all there. Maybe they find a small house in North Ryde for $520,000. It's not what they dreamed of, but it's all they can afford.

After expenses, they have $360,000 left to invest. Where to invest it? It's too late for super and at this stage in their lives they are looking for a sure, steady income, so shares are too volatile. They invest it in a conservative managed fund that will average 6 per cent per annum, over a minimum of five years. This generates an extra $21,600 before tax each year. After tax they will have $20,000 from the managed fund. So they are living on $38,000 per annum. Admittedly not in the house they wanted to live in, but at least they can survive. In fact, they can now afford the 'must haves' list.

What happens with a plan?

Let's imagine our couple decide to create an investment plan. With experienced and professional advice and information, they agree on an effective plan of action, involving a budget, paying off the family home earlier and investing by using equity in the home and exchanging tax dollars for property. He earns a gross salary of $82,500. After tax, he is left with $56,000 a year.

Take one! The home is worth $450,000. They have only $100, 000 left on the mortgage, so they have $350,000 equity in their home. With that equity, having worked out the compelling future calculations, they decide to buy a new investment unit at Chatswood for $380,000. The total interest-only loan comes to $400,000, including fees, stamp duties, some insurances and a small amount of contingency to cover a vacancy period (which, I have found, is rarely needed, but does help many investors to sleep better!) Once they have settled, they will be able to use tax deductions to increase his take-home pay and offset most, if not all, of the expenses after rent.

They look at how they are paying off their own home and examine ways to bring this down, such as 'line of credit' loan accounts, paying the mortgage weekly or fortnightly and putting any extra money into the mortgage. This extra money is gained through restructuring their budget and reducing outgoings wherever possible – but without sentencing them to years of bread and water! Through this, many investors are normally able to work out ways of paying off the family home five years quicker.

When the home is paid off, the investment property loan can change to a 'principal and interest' loan and the original loan repayments for the family home are added to the loan payments on the investment loan. Fifteen years down the track, they have paid off their own home and their investment property and can retire with an investment property worth around $800,000 (a conservative estimate) and super funds of around $300,000. (These super funds, as I have already indicated, would give around $18,000 a year, tax-free, if placed in a government-approved roll-over pension or annuity at around 6 per cent return.)

If they then sell the property, after capital gains tax and sales expenses of around $150,000, they are left with a profit of around $650,000.

If they choose to invest the profit from the investment property in managed funds at 6 per cent return, this will give them an income of $39,000 a year. After tax this will be around $34,000 a year. They will be receiving $18,000 from his super, so will now have an approximate net yearly income of $52,000. Pretty good, but not quite up at the '*could haves*' level – yet.

Take Two! What if they choose not to sell and continue to hold the property and use the income from the rent as their investment return? If the property is worth around $800,000 the rent could be around the $850 a week mark. Once tax deductions have been made from the taxable rental income, such as maintenance costs, insurance, management fees and rates, and tax is paid on the reduced income after these deductions, the tax bill will be around $2,000 for the year. Once expenses have been paid out of around $11,000 for the year, the $850 a week gross rent becomes around $600 a week net. In other words, the net return from the total rental return would be around $30,000. This net income of $30,000 and the income from the super funds gives them $30,000 + $18,000. That's a total of $48,000 a year. Still nearly $20,000 short of the 'could haves' list.

Take Three! Now let's try again. This time they are going to calculate beforehand how to reach the nest egg of $1,287,000 using the plan of selling the property after they have retired. They already have $300,000 of this in their super fund so they need to find another $987,000. This is the profit they need to make on their property, after capital gains tax and sales costs.

Working backwards, in order to make such a profit they will need to sell a property at $1,200,000, which, after $227,000 has been deducted through capital gains tax and sales expenses, will give them $973,000 profit. To achieve this they will need to buy at around $600,000 in the first place. This will need a loan of $650,000. This loan will need to be paid back totally in the 15 years. If they can manage to pay out the loan, will this now guarantee them a place in the 'could haves' list?

If this profit of $973,000 is invested in managed funds at 6 per cent yearly return, it yields $58,380 a year before tax. This will be around $48,000 after tax. Add this to the $18,000 yearly income from the super and they will get $66,000. I'd say that was close enough!

However, look at the level of loan they have taken on for just one property. The problem is that the interest alone on a loan of $650,000 at 8 per cent is $1,000 a week. There will be only one rent coming in and only one set of deductions to claim from the property. Wouldn't it be more profitable to buy two properties for a slightly higher loan value, and get two rental incomes and two sets of deductions for slightly more than the price of one?

Take Four! Let's try this with two properties and see how the figures add up. Again, the couple choose to invest in a CBD like Sydney's Chatswood for higher capital returns and above-average rental yields. Again they begin by putting effort into paying off their own house as quickly as possible. They then buy their first property 'off the plan' for $420,000, with an interest-only loan of $440,000. Three years down the track, with increased equity in both their own home and in their first investment property, they buy their second property, again off the plan, in another new CBD development for $440,000, with an interest-only loan of $460,000. Two years after this, they have finished paying off their own home and change their loan on the first property to principle and interest. In this way, when they retire, they have paid off their own home, the first investment property and still have an interest-only loan on their second property.

The first property, on a conservative 6 per cent capital growth per annum, has risen in value to around $1,000,000 over 15 years. The second has at least doubled in value over 12 years to $880,000. Now they will sell both. The first will net them profits, after capital gains tax and sales costs, of $810,000. The second will generate less profit, since they will also pay out the original $460,000 loan. After expenses it will generate $255,000. With the $300,000 rolled over into a government-approved pension or annuity, their total nest egg on retirement will be

$300,000 + $910,000 + $255,000 = $1,465,000

With around $18,000 a year from the super and a 6 per cent yearly return of $69,900 on the profits from the investment properties, even after tax of around $14,000 a year, they will receive a net yearly income of around **$73,900.**

They will have made it with an extra $10,000 a year to work with! In the next chapter I'll demonstrate how they can actually afford to pay for this investment plan. It is a lot easier than many people realise.

APPRECIATING
A$$ETS

C H A P T E R   9

PAYING FOR
YOUR FUTURE

> "Most people fail to realise that in life it's not how much money
> you make, it's how much money you keep."
>
> Robert T. Kiyosaki

The quote above sums up one of the basic rules of successful investment. How can you increase the money that you keep for yourself, your investment plan, your future? Firstly, without the will,
there is no way. You will need the desire, the commitment and a clearly-
defined goal to do this. Without these elements firmly in place, the
money you save will waft out of your pockets and out the door as if by
magic!

Let's imagine you have come to me with a plan to invest in residential property and have gone through the compelling future calculations, as
in the previous chapter. Now the next stage is simple. I will ask you to
work out how much you spend each week — and then we will look at
ways to keep more of your money to pay off your debts and loans more
quickly and to increase your ownership of assets.

Why is this so important? In 23 years of observing wealthy people, I
have noticed one thing they all do:

They spend less than they earn!
What they save, they invest.

It really is that simple. Mr Micawber, in Charles Dickens' novel *David Copperfield* states this clearly. "Annual income twenty pounds, annual expenditure nineteen nineteen six, result happiness. Annual income twenty pounds, annual expenditure twenty pounds ought and six, result misery."

In other words, if your expenditure is a few cents more than your income, you are headed for unhappiness. This is a lesson that needs to be taught to children as soon as possible. If they grow up with this understanding then their chances of becoming wealthy are a hundred times that of their parents. If they start to invest for their future when young, even if it is just putting 10 per cent of their pocket money or earnings into a savings account, they will be considerably more wealthy than their poor parents, who either didn't learn, or learned much later in life, to spend less than they earned. Give them the big picture, the goal to aim for and the means of saving. To help them reach their goals, some parents I know offer to match dollar for dollar the amount they save.

Children are sponges and soak up everything we do. If they see their parents spending beyond their means, exhausting their credit cards and never saving, this is the model they will learn from and this is the example they will repeat. I believe parents have a duty to their children to set them positive and intelligent examples throughout life, and handling money is no exception.

Think about how much money you actually receive over, let's say, 40 years of working. Forty years of 52 pay packets a week is over 2,000 pay

Where did all the money go?

ARTCHA '02

packets. Why is it that so many 60 year-olds have only $5,000 in savings and no investments? Where did all that money go? Even if they had saved $20 a week from their wages, they would have at least $40,000 in savings – more if they had used the leverage of compound interest.

I have spent many years walking around with one of my greatest investments, a mini spiral-bound notebook that cost a dollar and has made me millions! I used this notebook to write down everything I spent. I mean everything! Every cup of coffee, every postage stamp, every newspaper. I will ask you to do the same, so that you can see how quietly and quickly money can disappear from your pocket. Whilst I was doing this, I even found myself not buying some things, because I was tired of writing them all down! The sad thing is in my experience, that even though I will ask you to do this, 99 per cent of people stop doing it within a week! Persevere! Be honest!

Once you have worked out how much you are spending, you can graduate from the notebook to an A–Z expanding file. Each week put enough money to cover all the fixed items of expenditure into this file. In 'E' for electricity, put enough in every week to cover the average weekly cost. To work out some of these expenses, look back at your last year's bills, total them up and divide them by 52 to find out how much you need to put in for a week. If your total expenditure on electricity was $940 last year, divide that by 52 and then put slightly more, to cover rising costs, into the file each week.

$$\$ \quad \frac{940}{52} \quad = \$18.08$$

So, round it up and put in $20 each week. Do the same with telephone, insurance, rates, groceries, petrol, car running costs, holiday costs, dry cleaning, maintenance on the house you live in, everything. Work out how much it costs a week, round it up and put that much per week into each of the sections in your file.

There is one new section that you must create. Mine is under 'D' for Downs! This is the section where each week you will put at least 10 per cent of your take-home pay or even better, at least 10 per cent of your gross pay. It is this section that you must pay first each week, before everything else! I now put in 30 per cent of my income. This is my investment money.

Eventually the physical practice of putting away your weekly amounts will become ingrained, like all habits. Your expenditures may look like the example below from George and Jenny Harrison, clients who are now about to buy their first investment property.

George and Jenny

George, 38, earns $69,000 a year gross salary. Jenny, 35, works part-time and earns $26,700 a year gross. They have three children and owe $92,000 on their family home, now worth around $500,000. I immediately ask them to start putting aside 10 per cent of their income into the 'H' for Harrison account. This money would be useful in paying off their home loan quicker and so, with no delay, an extra $140 on top of the existing $200 is paid off against the remains of their existing home loan.

Line of credit accounts. Another way in which to maximise their income is to choose their type of loan account carefully. If they choose to open a 'line of credit' account, which many banks and financial institutions now have, they will be saving themselves money every time they put their income in and any extra money, even if they take part of it out later. This is how it can work. You organise to take out an equity-secured interest-only loan of $420,000 at 7.5 per cent interest. You are paying the interest on the full amount until you then deposit your income. For the time that the income stays in the account, you can withdraw part or all of it, but, as long as it is there, it has the effect of reducing the amount that you owe and you pay interest on the reduced amount. You are then able to save $1,000 a month. This goes into your line of credit. If you need it, you can withdraw it. As long as it is there, it also has the effect of reducing the loan amount and so reduces the interest you are paying.

If the Harrisons manage to pay off their own home before the term of the interest-only loan on their first property has finished, they can deposit the $520 they were paying off on their home loan each week into the line of credit account. Once the term of the interest-only loan is over, they can then change it to a principal and interest loan and use the $520 weekly to start paying this off. Each $520 that they deposit until then still has the effect of reducing their interest payments, so they are able to make this money work for them where they need it most.

They change their loan to a line of credit loan, where whatever they put in at the beginning of the month helps to bring down the amount they owe, so decreasing the amount of interest they have to pay. Any income, overtime, bonuses or extra cash goes into it, as well as their savings. They put all their expenses on a credit card and then withdraw from the loan at the end of the month to pay off the credit card, before the 'interest-free' period on their purchases expires. In this way they can keep their interest payments as low as possible with no extra cost to them. The extra $140 a week will also reduce the amount of interest by reducing the amount they owe in total (the principal) more quickly. In this way they will pay thousands less in interest to the bank, increase their equity in the family home faster – and have paid it off years sooner.

Gross income (joint)	$ 95,700
Net income (joint)	$ 71,500
Weekly income (joint)	$ 1,375
Weekly expenditure	
'H' for Harrison (10% of net)	$ 140
Loan repayments	$ 200
Electricity	$ 35
Telephone, inc. mobiles	$ 40
Insurance – 2 cars	$ 40
Insurance – house and contents	$ 20
Car maintenance	$ 45
Petrol	$ 60
Council rates and water rates	$ 45
School expenses	$ 40
Pre-school fees	$ 60
Groceries	$ 180
Clothing and shoes	$ 50
Newspapers and magazines	$ 25
Wine/beer	$ 40
Eating out/lunches & dinners	$ 120
Babysitting fees	$ 30
Personal grooming	$ 30
Dry-cleaning	$ 15
Take away foods	$ 40
Excursions and holidays	$ 75
Miscellaneous, gifts etc	$ 40
Total expenditure	$ 1,370

With $340 a week now being paid off against the home loan, the Harrisons will still have trouble paying off their home loan as quickly as they would like.

Looking at this list, I have asked them to work out how they can cut the expenditure down, without causing too much impact on their lifestyle. They have come up with some suggestions and have agreed to put them into practice immediately. They will put into effect a process of 'shaving' some of their non-essential costs. Through only eating out once every two weeks, rather than every week, through making takeaways into a once a week treat, dropping a magazine each, not spending so much on clothes, buying less processed and prepared foods, drinking less alcohol, taking lunches to work and planning a cheaper holiday each year, their new expenditure list now looks like this.

Weekly expenditure

'H' for Harrison (10% of net)	$ 140
Loan repayments	$ 200
Electricity	$ 35
Telephone/mobiles	$ 40
Insurance – 2 cars	$ 40
Insurance – house and contents	$ 20
Car maintenance costs	$ 45
Petrol	$ 60
Council rates and water rates	$ 45
School expenses	$ 40
Preschool fees	$ 60
Groceries	$ 160
Clothing and shoes	$ 40
Newspapers and magazines	$ 20
Wine/beer	$ 30
Eating out/lunches & dinners	$ 50
Babysitting fees	$ 15
Personal grooming	$ 20
Dry-cleaning	$ 15
Take away foods	$ 25
Excursions and holidays	$ 60
Miscellaneous, gifts etc	$ 30
Total expenditure	**$ 1,190**

This now leaves them with an extra $180 to add to their existing $340 to pay off their loan. $520 a week will pay out their home loan in less than four years and save them thousands in interest payments.

In the meantime, they will now look at how much they need to invest to give them their financial goals on retirement. They have worked out that they will buy two properties, one now and one in four year's time. The first property will be on an interest-only loan until the family home is paid off. Then it will change to a principal and interest loan and the loan repayment amounts will go to paying off the first investment property. At this stage they will buy the second property.

How much investment will they need?

With the total super for the couple at retirement in 22 years being estimated at $400,000, the Harrisons will need around another $1,000,000 in profit on their properties in 22 years to create an adequate nest egg. The properties need to have a value of around $1,200,000 PLUS the amount outstanding on the two property loans to create $1,000,000 profit. Let's say they need a total gross value on the two properties of $1,800,000. It sounds a lot, but they have some time on their side. In 22 years property values will have at least tripled. If the Harrisons buy their first property at around $400,000 with a $420,000 loan, it will be worth at least $1,200,000 on their retirement. If they buy their second property four years later at $450,000, with a loan of $475,000, it will be worth at least $1,000,000 on their retirement. By the time they retire they will have paid off the first property.

On its sale, and after expenses, the first property will give a total profit of around $970,000. The second property will give, after the loan has been paid out and sales expenses, profit of around $360,000. This gives a total profit of around $1,330,000.

Now they invest this profit in managed funds at an average 6 per cent return. Their super will be returning $24,000 a year, tax free, because it has been rolled over into a government-approved annuity or pension. Their managed funds will be giving them around $80,000 pre-tax. That's around $63,000 after tax. Their total net yearly income on retirement will be around $87,000!

How will they afford to put this plan into action? How will they be able to afford the interest repayments on the loans and all the expenses for the investment properties? Read on!

C H A P T E R   1 0

ASK THE TAX OFFICE FOR MONEY!

"In this world nothing can be said to be
more certain, except death and taxes."

Benjamin Franklin

Y ou're taxed when you earn. You're taxed when you spend. You're
taxed when you save. You're taxed when you die. Despite this, the
current taxation laws are attempting to encourage those who
wish to become self-funded retirees through tax deductions on investment expenses. But don't worry, the government hasn't gone all soft and
fuzzy. Whatever tax deductions you can claim now will be clawed back,
in part at least, by capital gains tax when you sell your investment assets!
But that's okay. The system works to enable you to invest NOW and to
reap the tax deduction benefits that will enable you to increase your
investment leverage NOW. And NOW is when you most need it!

What deductions?

I have already mentioned some of the deductions possible for equity
investments. These include tax deductions on franked dividends from
shares and the share components of managed funds, brokers' fees and
management fees; the ability to write off capital losses against capital gains

at a later date and interest on loans taken out to invest in equity invest-ments. When it comes to property, the deductions are comprehensive.

When you buy a residential investment property, the deductions begin with conveyancing fees, bank fees on setting up the loan, interest payable (but NOT the principal), accountancy, quantity surveyor, body corporate, property management and inspection report fees, rates, water rates and insurance costs. This is before the tenant has even moved in!

Some of these deductions are one-offs, but the ongoing fees, such as rates, interest and insurance, will continue as deductions for the years that you own the property and rent it out. Should you decide to move in yourself, the property is no longer deemed as an investment property and you lose the deductions from the date the property is taken off the rental market, or the date that you move in (whichever comes first). Then there are the deductions for the costs of repair and depreciation to the building and the fixtures and fittings.

Repairs can be deducted if they are made to restore the property to its original condition when you bought it. So putting in a spa bath can-not be claimed, since it is an improvement. You can claim it against your capital gains tax on selling the property, since it has added to the capital value of the property, but not now. If the spa bath that was there when you bought the property needs replacing, this counts as a repair and so can be used as a legitimate tax deduction. If you are not sure, ask your accountant. After all, you can deduct the accountant's fee too!

Depreciation

Building depreciation is calculated against the construction cost of the building, not against what you have paid for it. Currently at 2.5 per cent, this depreciation can be claimed each year. When you sell the build-ing it will be added up and will be part of the amount liable for capital gains tax. Still, better to have it now, if it helps pay for your investment in the first place. Besides, after 15 years, inflation will have eaten into its cur-rent value and the capital gains tax is only 50 per cent of what you claimed in the first place.

Fixture, fitting and furniture depreciation is calculated in a different way. As with the majority of these so-called 'assets', the Australian Tax Office (ATO) recognises that they lose value over time. So you can claim depreciation on their cost. The cost is calculated to include, where appli-cable, a small percentage of architect fees, installation costs, transportation costs and other associated costs. The cost of the dishwasher, for example, will factor in these 'hidden' costs on top of the actual price of the dishwasher. Again, consult the experts. The quantity surveyor will include these costs in the written value as the survey is done. The ATO has worked out the 'effective life' of all items eligible for depreciation. You can go with this or determine your own 'effective life' figure.

There are two ways of calculating this depreciation. In prime cost depreciation, 100 per cent of the initial value is divided by this 'effective life' figure to give you a figure that you can claim as depreciation each year. As an example, if that dishwasher has an effective life of seven years, for seven years you can claim 14.3 per cent of the value of the dishwasher as part of the total depreciation.

$$\frac{100\%}{7} = 14.3\%$$

So, if the value of the dishwasher is $800, you will be able to claim $114.40 (14.3 per cent x $800) every year for seven years.

The other method is to claim diminishing value depreciation. This diminishing percentage is calculated using the same effective life figure, but dividing it into 150 per cent of the designated value of the item.

$$\frac{150\%}{7} = 21.43\%$$

At the end of year one, you can claim $171.44 (21.43 per cent x $800). The value of the item then diminishes by the amount claimed, changing its value to $628.56 ($800 - $171.44). At the end of year two, you can claim $134.70 (21.43 per cent x $628.56). The value of the item then diminishes by the amount claimed, changing its value to $493.86 ($628.56 - $134.70)

And so on, and so forth. Unless you enjoy these calculations, I suggest you get your accountant to work out the figures and to suggest which method is the most efficient financially.

Basically, the tax deductions can be divided into four areas. These are

- Initial purchase and set-up expenses
- Ongoing rental expenses
- Ongoing interest payment
- Ongoing depreciations of building, fixtures and fittings.

When can you claim them? You could wait until the end of each tax year to claim these deductions and get a tax refund, or you could ask the ATO to alter your tax rate immediately. In this way, the benefit of tax deductions starts when you need it most, not 15 months down the track. The ATO can issue (under Section 15-15) an acceptance of your request to 'vary' your existing tax rate to take into account the new expenses you have taken on through property investment. Either apply through your accountant or get the correct forms from the ATO and fill them in yourself. Personally, I get my accountant to do them. It takes a quarter of the time — and I am confident that if it is left to the experts there will be no hold ups or mistakes in setting up the new tax rates.

Through the issue of this variation of your tax rate, paying for your investment becomes a little easier, since you will have more in your weekly pay packet to offset the extra costs generated by such investments. Let's have a look at how this will affect the Harrisons.

The first investment property that they buy is in George's name as he earns nearly three times as much as his wife. His gross salary is $69,000. He has been paying $19,810 in tax a year, leaving him with $49,190 in his hand. The first investment property that they buy is $400,000 and for this purchase they take out an interest-only loan of $420,000 at 7.8 per cent over four years. They let this property for $420 a week.

The property expenses of $5460 are estimated based on about 25 per cent of the total rent ($21,840) received for the year. The interest payments for the year are $32,760 ($420,000 x 7.8 per cent).

For the first year George's tax situation changes as follows:

New income ($69,000 salary + $21,840 rent) $ 90,840

Rental deductions from gross income
Interest $ 32,760
Property expenses $ 5,460
Depreciation on building (2.5 per cent x $200,000) $ 5,000
Depreciation of fittings (various calculations) $ 7,200
Borrowing costs (initial fees on purchase) $ 1,800

Total deductions   **$ 52,220**

New taxable income ($90,840 – $52,220)   **$ 38,620**

Tax on $38,620   **$ 7,966**

Now let's look at their total income and their expenditure

Income		Expenditure	
George's salary	$ 69,000	George's tax	$ 7,966
Jenny's salary	$ 26,700	Jenny's tax	$ 4,390
Rent	$ 21,840	Loan repayment	$ 27,040
		Interest repayment	$ 32,760
Total	**$ 117,540**	Rental expenses	$ 5,460
		Living expenses	$ 40,560
		Total	**$ 118,176**

They are $636 short. Back to the budget! They need to shave another $12 a week off their expenditure. They agree to shave $5 off their eating out allowance, $5 off the miscellaneous section and $2 off the personal grooming allowance per week. Made it!

In the following three years, things will remain relatively similar. Even if they did have three or four weeks each year with no rent, the extra few thousand they borrowed on the loan acts as a buffer.

At the start of the fifth year their circumstances change, when they borrow to buy another rental property. They have also managed to pay off their own home, releasing $540 a week for loan repayments. This money can be put into paying off a new principal and interest loan on the first property. Their salaries have gone up a little. Their living expenses have gone up a little too. Their rent has gone up a little and now they have a new set of figures to recalculate where they stand.

Here we go again!

Jenny's gross salary is now $29,200. She is paying $5,140 in tax. George's gross salary is now $76,000. The second residential investment property that they buy is $450,000 and for this purchase they take out an interest-only loan of $475,000 at 8.8 per cent over four years. They let this property for $460 a week. The rent on the first property is now up to $450 a week. For this calculation, we will assume they had tenants in both properties for 50 weeks of the year.

The rental expenses can be estimated at $11,375 or 25 per cent of the total rent received for the year ($45,500 x 25 per cent).

The new principal and interest loan for the first property is 8 per cent, fixed for five years. The interest payments for the first year will be

$33,600 ($420,000 x 8 per cent). Interest payments for the second property are $41,800 ($475,000 x 8.8 per cent). Total interest payments are $75,400 ($33,600 + $41,800). The living expenses have gone up by, say, 10 per cent to become $44,616

For the fifth year, George's tax situation changes as follows:

New income ($76,000 salary + $45,500 rent) $ 121,500

Rental deductions from gross income

Interest	$ 75,400
Property expenses	$ 11,375
Depreciation on building #1 (2.5 per cent x $200,000) $	5,000
Depreciation of fittings #1 (various calculations)	$ 7,200
Borrowing costs #2 (initial fees on purchase)	$ 2,100
Depreciation on building #2 (2.5 per cent x $240,000) $	6,000
Depreciation of fittings 2# (various calculations)	$ 8,200
Total deductions	$ 115,275

New taxable income ($121,500 – $115,275) $ 6,225

Tax on $6,225 $ 40

Now let's look at their total income and their expenditure

Income		Expenditure	
George's salary	$ 76,000	George's tax	$ 40
Jenny's salary	$ 29,200	Jenny's tax	$ 5,140
Rent	$ 45,500	Interest payments	$ 75,400
Total	**$ 150,700**	Rental expenses	$ 11,375
		Living expenses	$ 44,616
		Total	**$ 136,571**

The surplus $14,129 for the year will be paid into the principal and interest loan on property #1 to reduce the principal and so bring down the interest in the following year.

If they wanted to, they could easily afford to do it all again in another couple of years!

How to sleep better at night!

Once you have decided on investing in a residential property, how can you ensure that your decision carries the least risk possible? Risk minimisation is a built-in part of the game play of all financially intelligent investors. Adequate insurance can work much better than sleeping pills! There is no investment in the world worth having if it makes you sick with worry.

Investors need to insure both the investment property and its contents and fittings. They are also expected to take out landlord protection insurance. The fear that a tenant might damage a property, or leave unexpectedly owing rent is a common fear that all rental property investors have entertained at some point. Landlord protection insurance is a safeguard against this. It also covers loss of rent if the property was made uninhabitable through fire or water damage.

Financially intelligent investors need to have some sort of mortgage and income insurance, so that an accident or illness will not mean the loss of their investment or any risk to their ability to pay out the loan. Death cover is also expected. Financially intelligent investors update their wills so that the investment property is properly disposed of in the event of the investor's death. You need to set up these insurance policies before settlement, so that they are covered immediately settlement occurs.

The costs of some of these insurance policies can be factored into the property loan and the loan repayments so that investors do not have to find all the insurance costs up front. The same applies to application fees, solicitor's fees, stamp duty and inspection fees. The investor will need to update or make a will and take out death cover and income protection insurance.

Property management

If you are investing individually and do not have the time, talent or inclination to manage the property yourself (which is most of us!) you must shop around for a good property manager. Choose one local to the investment property and choose one from a reputable real estate agent. If you are not sure of their reputation, look for information. Ask them how many rental properties they have on their books and what sort of vacancy rates these properties have been averaging. If they have no figures to give you, look elsewhere.

Ask how often they do property inspections. They can do this up to four times a year, as long as adequate notice is given to the tenants. Ask how long the property manager has been working in their current position. There can be a high turnover of staff with some estate agents, which means you do not get a chance to establish a relationship with the property manager and there is little consistency of service. Finally, if you are not happy with the one you have employed, approach the overall manager of the estate agent and talk directly to them. You can always take your business elsewhere.

After settlement

So the bank has coughed up the money – and the property has been finished or vacated, depending on whether you are buying a newly-built property or an older property. The first task of the investor after settlement is to fill in a final inspection report before the tenant moves in. With a brand new property any cracks, breaks or faults need to be passed on to the property manager. If the problem is not rectified immediately, the investor will need to monitor the progress of repairs at the six monthly or yearly inspections. If cracks in the wall have appeared as the building starts to settle, it is likely that the developer will want to wait for the building to settle completely before fixing them. I recommend to investors that they make a list of all repairs needed and take photographs. The lists and photographs can be passed on to their solicitor for action.

Once the final inspection report is signed and passed on to the property manager, the tenant will receive a copy that they too must complete and sign, stating if they agree or disagree with the report on the condition of the property as they move in. They normally have 14 days from the start of the tenancy to do this.

Another inspection to be done is the quantity survey. In this survey, a quantity surveyor will list all fittings and their values, from carpets to door handles. This survey, which costs the investor approximately $500, is then passed on to you or your accountant and used to calculate the value and depreciation on both building and contents and fittings for tax purposes (see the beginning of this chapter.)

Now all you have to do is sit back and let time and leverage work their magic for your retirement! As Robert T Kiyosaki writes, "It's like planting a tree. You water it for years and then one day it doesn't need you any more. Its roots have gone down deep enough. Then the tree provides shade for you enjoyment."

YOU'VE MADE IT, NOW HOLD ON TO IT!

O ne of the biggest mistakes that people make on retirement is that they stop paying themselves that 10 per cent minimum from their retirement income. If George and Jenny want to stay one step ahead of inflation and create a buffer, so that their investment can remain intact to pass on to their nearest and dearest when that other inevitable thing happens, they would be wise to take 10 per cent of their income and invest it.

$$10\% \times \$87,000 = \$8,700$$

At around 6 per cent return, in 10 years they will have around $114,675. Plenty for the new Porsche! Or wait for 20 years and have enough to afford a full-time housekeeper, a gardener and a chauffeur!

Even if you are living on less than $25,000 a year from your super and a part-pension, I still advise that you pay yourself first. Earlier in the book, I mentioned a friend of mine who is on a very low income, but still manages to save by putting all the coins in her purse at the end of the day into a money box. Even these small amounts add up and, with compound interest in an income-producing managed fund, can help to offset inflation and create an emergency fund.

As mentioned earlier, managed funds come in different packages. At this time in your life, where you need income yield more than capital growth and tax offsets, a conservative fund such as a money-market fund is more appropriate to generate a monthly income. This gives you choice, security and convenience.

Sell! Sell! Sell!

Why do I tell most of my clients to sell their investment properties at retirement? I see property simply as a vehicle for investment that gives fairly predictable growth. Even if the returns are lower than those of shares held over the long term, property is not as volatile. If purchased correctly in a prime position and set up correctly with a prime tenant and effective financing, my experience has been that property as a vehicle for investment is relatively easy to manage. In this way we can get on with our lives whilst the investment grows over time.

I have been involved in the real estate industry for nearly 25 years now and have observed closely what works and what does not work when it comes to selling property. Whether you are selling a family home or an investment property, the mechanics of successful selling are the same.

I have witnessed countless people putting themselves through emotional turmoil and major fallouts with family and professionals when trying to sell their properties because they were unrealistic about both process and outcome. The first rule is:

If you are selling, be prepared to sell!

Let me explain. When you decide to sell your property, be it family home or investment property, you will probably choose a real estate agent to do this. You can expect the agent to attract buyers to your property through various means. You can expect the agent to ask the potential buyers for offers on your property. You can then expect them to come to you with these offers for your consideration. It is then YOUR JOB to accept or reject what the potential purchaser thinks your property is worth in the current market.

Most people think estate agents sell real estate. They don't. YOU DO! Estate agents find buyers, ask for offers and submit these offers to you. **You accept or reject. You either sell or don't sell.** Both you and the agent have a common goal, to realise the best possible price in the current market for your property. You are both looking to gain maximum profit. They are working on commission. You need the maximum profit to achieve maximum dollars for investment to achieve maximum income for retirement. Teamwork is essential. Also essential is an understanding of how the buyers' market works.

In any marketplace there are a range of properties at a range of prices in one area. Some are dress circle properties, some are middle of the road and some are cheap. There may also be a small number of properties that are "to die for". I call them "WOW" properties. Some buyers will be looking at the cheapies, some in the middle and some will be looking in the dress circle price range. A lucky few will be looking at the WOW properties.

Let's consider a suburb in your town and put some hypothetical prices on the range of properties available.

Cheapies –	up to $ 200,000
Middle range –	$ 200,000 – $ 450,000
Dress-circle -	$ 450,000 – $ 600,000
WOW -	more than $ 600,000

In my time I have noticed that around three per cent of the population in most centres in this country are in buy/sell mode at any one time. Let's say that your suburb or town has 5,000 properties.

3% of 5,000 = 150

If the average time taken to sell a property is around three months, then 150 people will be buying in that area over three months. These 150 hypothetical buyers will be spread over the range of prices.

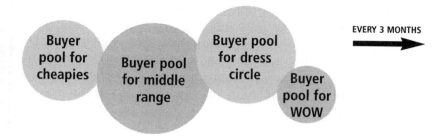

If we look at what that buyer pool of 150 every three months can afford, we would probably get a breakdown something like this:

40 can afford the cheapies
90 can afford the middle range
15 can afford the dress circle
 5 can afford WOW

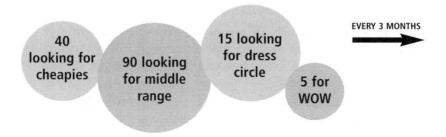

Something else is important to remember at this stage.

Buyers usually spend more than they plan to!

Most buyers want to buy UP to the next level. The cheapies want to live in the middle range, the middle range really want dress circle and the dress circle aspire to WOW! It's like buying a burger! If people are offered a drink or fries for a little bit extra they will often say yes and spend a bit more to get more. This psychology is so predictable that sales staff at fast food places are trained to automatically 'prompt' buyers into buying more than they thought they wanted!

In the case of the buyer pool, this means many buyers end up in the next pool when they are prompted to look at how much more they will get for just a bit extra. If you put a realistic price on your property in the first place and choose an agent who understands their part of the bargain – finding as many potential buyers as possible, you are able to tap into a larger part of the buyer pool and so increase your chances of selling quickly and profitably.

Ask your agent to give you a breakdown of how they will attract buyers from each pool and what they will be doing to earn the money they will make from your sale.

Listen to the offers that come in. If they are all well below your asking price, are you asking the right price? Often the best offers come within 30 days of going on the market. If you want to sell the property quickly then be prepared to listen to the buyers and take into account what they are willing to pay on the day.

In my experience advertising your property with no price attached works best. This can be done by advertising it for auction or by a system called 'Buyer Range Selling' developed by Dave Pilling in Adelaide and Perth. This puts your property in a price range so that buyers from all buyer pools are encouraged to look at your property. The cheapies will look at the lower end of the price range and go for that. The middle range and dress circle will look at the higher end of the price range and think it might be a possibility too!

All will come to view the property and someone will fall in love with it! If you are going to go fishing, it doesn't matter how tasty your bait is if there are no fish in the pool to bite!

Buyer Range Selling does work. I have tried it many times and have found it very successful.

I could write another book on selling, but suffice to say that you will stay sane, happy and wealthy if you follow these simple rules.

1. YOU sell your property. Agents only find buyers.
2. Every property market has many different price ranges.
3. There are buyers in every price range.
4. Most buyers spend more than they mean to!
5. If you put a set price on your property, you can only move down from there and you may miss out on many potential buyers who see the price as out of their buying range.
6. Try to stay calm if your agent is not bringing in the offers you want. Remember, they only get paid if you ACCEPT an offer, so it is in their interest to try to get offers you'll accept.
7. What you think your property is worth is rarely correct! Listen to the buyers. They are probably more familiar with what's available on the market than you are.
8. Try to sell in the first 30 days, when the interest is at its peak and the buyer pool is at its freshest and fullest.
9. Keep a grip on your emotions. Sentimental attachments are costly in the property market and getting angry or upset solves nothing.

When it comes to selling investment property, if you bought with good advice and a sound financial plan, then you will almost certainly make a good profit. Imagine that you purchased a property in 1995 for $300,000 and then wanted to sell in 2010 for $700,000. How much difference would it make to your investment plans if you actually accepted an offer of $690,000 or even $680,000? In terms of yearly income it might mean you get five dollars a week less! Can you live with that?

Your expectations on how much you will get on sale of your property are the most important part of the selling experience. If you are unrealistic – and I have found this to be the most common problem encountered in selling properties – selling can become a nightmare battle between you and the agent. If you make sure you understand what the current market price is when you decide to sell your property and set no price or a price range, you will save yourself much angst, worry and frustration as well as time.

It's sold! Now what?

In retirement our needs change. Now we want the safest course of action that will give us some capital growth, but emphasises the priority of a living income over growth. I suggest managed funds or allocated pensions for this purpose.

There is also another vehicle that may be appropriate at this stage of life. For those of you who want to continue with property investment, it can be very good at generating an income through rent, if the site is chosen with your new needs in mind.

Capital growth versus income

Prime CBD residential real estate is my pre-retirement investment vehicle of choice. Once I retire I will be looking for something other than the high capital growth I used to build up my investments. I will be looking for higher rental yields to give me an income. The tax deductions will no longer be playing a major part in my investments and so the expenses become more of a liability than before because I will have no wage from work to offset against them.

How I work out rental yields is simple. I divide the rent by the rental expenses. For a prime property in the CBD of Sydney, the expenses will be higher than a property in Dubbo, a city in the New England region of NSW. Rates will be higher in the CBD. The management fee will be higher. Body Corporate fees, insurance, maintenance will all cost more in the CBD. Replacing expensive fittings as they wear with the years becomes a drain on retirement income. Yes, the capital growth is still there, but it is not useful to me in generating income. I can only get hold of it if I sell. I need the rent to be a main part of my income on retirement. I'd like the expenses to be as low as possible.

Why Dubbo? It is a city referred to by Bernard Salt in his book *The Big Shift* as 'a sponge city'. Along with other cities like Tamworth, Lismore and Grafton, they soak up the young people from the surrounding towns and townships. This is where the employment is. This is where young people are moving to. In the period over 1976 to 2000, Dubbo's population grew by nearly 58 per cent! Outlying communities around Dubbo, such as Gilgandra, Coolah and Wellington lost 10 to 15 per cent of their population (Bernard Salt *The Big Shift* KPMG).

Where there is population growth and young people moving in, there is scope for residential property investment. It has the advantage of higher rental yields, more properties for your money and a need for rental properties.

The flying doctor!

One of my clients is a doctor, now retired, who is a small-aviation pilot. He has his own plane and wants to spend his retirement flying. This costs a lot of money. He had a portfolio of several prime Sydney CBD properties. On retirement he wanted to stay with property as his investment vehicle. He wasn't interested in shares or managed funds.

We worked out how much income was needed to fund his lifestyle. The rents from his CBD properties were good, but not quite enough. If he was to sell his CBD properties and buy in a small city like Lismore, Grafton or Dubbo, he could afford more than three times the number of properties and would get more total rent than with his CBD ones. The capital growth of properties in one of theses cities would not be as much as in the CBD, but he needed income now, not capital growth. The actual worth of his total investments would be the same, but more of that worth would be sitting in his pocket now, because he was getting more rent, at the sacrifice of capital growth.

He sold his CBD properties and, with the profits, bought several small blocks of flats in Dubbo and Tamworth. The rental yield on these flats came to 12 per cent, enough to generate the income he needed for successful retirement. The money he made through capital growth in the

CBD was used to buy enough properties in these 'sponge' cities to create a wealthy lifestyle for him. He even enjoyed inspecting the properties. It gave him an excuse to fly more often!

Sydney CBD property		Dubbo property	
Currently worth	$ 615,000	Currently worth	$ 215,000
Bought for (a year ago)	$ 560,000	Bought for (a year ago)	$ 205,000
Capital growth	**9.5%**	**Capital growth**	**4.5%**
Rental yield	$\frac{\$520}{\$130} = 4\%$	**Rental yield**	$\frac{\$210}{\$25} = 8.4\%$
Total return	**13.5%**	**Total return**	**12.9%**

As you can see, there is not much difference in the total returns. The difference is in the amount of growth and yield. On retirement you need minimum expenses and maximum rent. If you bought the same value of property in Dubbo as you had in Sydney's CBD, what happens to your rental income and your expenses?

Sydney CBD		Dubbo	
One property	$ 560,000	3 properties	$ 560,000
Rental income	**$ 520** a week	Rental income	**$ 580** a week
Expenses	**$ 130** a week	Expenses	**$ 70** a week
Total income	**$ 390** a week	Total income	**$ 510** a week

Over a year this adds up to over $6,000 difference in rental income. He has bought a total of five small properties, giving him rent from 25 units and flats. This generates around $2,500 gross a week. Expenses and repairs can be claimed against his tax bill. He has chosen property because he dislikes shares and managed funds.

There are still tax implications and tenancy issues to consider with property. Many of my clients are happier to sell and reinvest the money in managed funds, annuities or pensions, so that they can enjoy their retirement knowing their money is being managed for them. Others like to have more direct management of their nest eggs. The choice is yours, and that is an important point! If you work towards your goals with financial intelligence and patience, you will have that choice at the end!

Meet the families – again!

It is time to go back to the families introduced in Chapter 3 and see how they will fare in retirement. For these families, I have assumed, optimistically, that the age pension will still be operating in 16 years time, and will be working under a similar structure to the current one. I have also assumed that the tax system will be similar then to the system we work under now.

After you have read about the families' outcomes on retirement, I'll ask you to consider, what if the pension is no longer there? In Chapter 1, I mentioned that future trends indicate the age pension is not something you can take for granted in your plans for retirement in fifteen or twenty years time. This is the reason you need to plan and start action on your financial independence NOW.

The Brownlows

Remember the Brownlows? Their motto is "She'll be right!" They subscribed to the belief that the government would take care of them. Where will they be in 16 years? We will assume an average yearly inflation rate of 4 per cent. We will also be optimistic and assume there is still an aged pension available.

At retirement they will have finally managed to pay off their family home. It will be worth around $1,100,000. They have decided to take out their $300,000 super as a lump sum and put it into a retirement fund, which is simply a specialised managed fund aimed at higher returns and lower growth. This, in itself, is a good thing. What is not good is that, by taking it as a lump sum, they will be taxed at 15 per cent. They will also now be taxed on the returns. If they had rolled it over to a government-approved annuity or pension, they would not have been taxed at the rollover stage, nor would they be taxed on the returns. What did they base their decision on? They saw an advert in the paper and thought it sounded like a good idea! The fund claimed to have higher interest and lower management fees than other funds.

So, after tax, they invest $245,000 in the retirement fund. They spend $10,000 on that cruise they have always promised themselves, as a reward for all their hard work. The fund gives them around 7 per cent per annum return. They will now receive just over $17,000 a year. If we take the current (2002) Centrelink pension and apply to it the 4 per cent inflation rate over 16 years and then take into account the income test, they will receive around $480 a week as a couple in part pension. They will also receive around $320 a week from their investment fund. This gives them a grand total of $800 a week. Tax would probably be negligible. In today's figures that is about $400 a week to live on. How much will this buy them?

Sticking to today's figures, they can afford $400 a week. They have only one car now, which helps to reduce costs.

Average weekly expenditure

Home maintenance	$ 20
Rates	$ 35
House and contents insurance	$ 20
Car insurance and green slip	$ 15
Car maintenance	$ 15
Petrol	$ 25
Electricity	$ 25
Telephone	$ 20
Groceries	$ 135
Clothes, shoes	$ 15
Eating out	$ 40
Books, papers, magazines	$ 15
Miscellaneous, gifts etc	$ 20
Total expenditure	**$ 400**

That's all folks! Look at their lifestyle. They can afford the basics, plus newspapers, the occasional book and dinner at the club once a week. Woe betide them if they are smokers or drinkers! There's no money left for that. They would have to give up other things to afford such expensive tastes. Private health cover? Can't afford it. Let's hope the government still provides an adequate public health service. Forget having a holiday, or even going to the cinema! What happens if the fridge breaks down? What about buying another car when the one they have is 10 years older? Where is the lifestyle they wanted? All they will have is a constant struggle to make the money go far enough.

They are poorer now than when they were working. This is something many people take for granted, that they will lead a poorer life in retirement. It doesn't have to be that way! If you choose to be wealthy and start now, you can achieve that wealth on retirement. Wouldn't that be a more fitting end to decades of hard work!

The Millers

So how will the Miller family fare on their retirement? Although they did take steps during their working lives to secure an investment for their future, their fear of debt prevented them from using the leverage of other people's money. They were in their mid 40s when they began their investment plan. They want to retire when Steven is 62 and Michelle is 60. According to current rules regarding age pensions, they will not be eligible for the age pension until they are 65. They will be dependent on their super and their investment returns for several years.

They have decided to sell the unit they own on retirement and esti-mate it will be worth around $225,000. After they sell it and pay off expenses such as capital gains tax and sales costs, they will be left with around $178,000. They will invest this in a conservative managed fund at around 6 per cent return per annum. This will net them around $10,700 each year. They also will rollover Steven's $300,000 super into a govern-ment-approved pension, giving them around $18,000 a year. In total they will receive $28,700 a year, around $550 a week. In 16 years time, though, that $550 a week will be the equivalent of around $280 a week in today's value once you have taken an average annual inflation rate of 4 per cent. Ouch! How can they survive on that?

Steven will have to wait until he is 65 to retire. Then they will be eligible for a part-pension (presuming it is still around and the govern-ment adjusts the assets test to keep pace with inflation). Optimistically their situation will change when Steven reaches 65. Michelle will still have two years to wait. If the pension remains and is index-linked to keep pace with inflation, he will receive around $450 a week. This will boost their income to around $1,000 a week. This, in today's money is around $500 a week. So the Millers will be able to spend $100 (in today's value) more than the Brownlows. They will be able to afford a little extra. Perhaps a trip to the cinema every week and a fortnight's holiday some-where in Australia once a year. Once Michelle becomes eligible for the pension this will boost their income again by around $100 a week, in today's values, to $600. They will be able to afford private health cover now. Hardly a wealthy lifestyle. If they had only used leverage to increase their investment earning potential, as the Turners and the Carringtons did, they would have a lot more to look forward to than 14 nights on the Sunshine Coast once a year, after all their hard work.

Average weekly expenditure

Home maintenance	$ 20
Rates	$ 35
House and contents insurance	$ 20
Car insurance and green slip	$ 15
Car maintenance	$ 15
Petrol	$ 25
Electricity	$ 25
Telephone	$ 20
Groceries	$ 130
Clothes, shoes	$ 20
Eating out, cinema, etc.	$ 70
Books, papers, magazines	$ 20
Private health cover	$ 30
Miscellaneous, gifts etc	$ 20
Holiday	$ 40
Total expenditure	**$ 505**

The Turners

The Turner family started from the same place as the Millers and the Brownlows. The difference was that they sought professional advice and also talked to people who had the experience of successful investment. The first part of their investment plan was to buy a CBD apartment for $380,000. For this they borrowed on the $350,000 equity in their own home and took out an interest-only loan for $400,000. They also put into place a budget and paid off the $100,000 still owing on their own house in seven years. They did not change to a principal and interest loan but put the extra money into a managed share portfolio. By the time they wanted to retire, at 60, they will have around $300,000 in super, a managed share fund with around $260,000 and a residential investment worth around $1,000,000.

They will sell the investment property, leaving them with a profit of around $410,000 after capital gains tax, sales costs and repayment of loan.

They will transfer the shares funds to a more conservative fund at around 6 per cent yearly return and will also add the $410,000 profit from the apartment sale. This will give them, including the rolled-over super of $300,000, a total investment figure of $970,000 at 6 per cent. This means they will not be eligible for an age pension, if it still exists. They will be living on an income of around $1,120 a week. After tax, this will be reduced to around $960 a week. Bearing in mind that this is the equivalent of around $480 a week in today's money, it is adequate, but not much more than that.

Average weekly expenditure

Home maintenance	$ 20
Rates	$ 35
House and contents insurance	$ 20
Car insurance and green slip	$ 15
Car maintenance	$ 15
Petrol	$ 25
Electricity	$ 25
Telephone	$ 20
Groceries	$ 130
Clothes, shoes	$ 20
Eating out, cinema, etc.	$ 60
Books, papers, magazines	$ 15
Private health cover	$ 30
Miscellaneous, gifts etc	$ 15
Holiday	$ 35
Total expenditure	**$ 480**

(Even though they are about par with the Millers, they do not have to worry about the fate of age pensions. If the pension is greatly reduced or non-existent, except for the lowest income brackets, then the Millers will be looking at around $270 a week in today's money from their super and managed funds.)

The Turners will be able to retire at 60, five years before the Millers and Brownlows because they are not dependent on government pension restrictions. They will be free of the worry about whether the pension will be around or will stay around once they have retired. If pensions do survive, they may even get a small part-pension once they reach 65 or they may reap benefits as the tax system is changed to encourage self-funded retirees, but they will not be dependent on it. They will be totally financially independent. If they had taken their plan one step further and gone for more than one property as their investment, creating further leverage as the Carringtons did, they could have done even better!

The Carringtons

The Carringtons did what the Turners did, except they did it again and again and again! They ended up with four investment properties! On retirement at 60, they will have amassed a total property asset value of around $4,000,000 and a total debt of $2,200,000. Once they have paid off the loans, the capital gains tax and the selling costs, they will have a profit of around $1,500,000. They will invest this in a managed fund at around 6 per cent per annum. They will roll-over their super of around $300,000, giving them a total weekly income of nearly $2,100!

After tax they will still have around $1,700 a week. This is the equivalent of about $850 a week in today's money. It looks like their retirement dreams of travelling to Africa and South America, of sailing, playing golf and learning to draw and paint will be turning into realities!

Average weekly expenditure

Home maintenance	$ 25
Rates	$ 35
House and contents insurance	$ 20
Car insurance and green slip	$ 15
Car maintenance	$ 15
Petrol	$ 30
Electricity	$ 25
Telephone	$ 20
Groceries	$ 160
Wines and spirits	$ 60
Clothes, shoes	$ 40
Eating out, cinema, etc.	$ 100
Books, papers, magazines	$ 25
Private health cover	$ 30
Miscellaneous, gifts etc	$ 30
Hobbies, clubs, sports	$ 100
Holiday	$ 120
Total expenditure	**$ 850**

Facing the future

I want you to consider the worst-case scenario now. What would happen to our families if the government had begun to phase out the age pension before they retired? For the Turners and Carringtons, both financially independent, it would not affect their income. For the Millers and the Brownlows it would be disastrous.

The Brownlows only have their super which will bring in around $346 a week. In today's money that is around $173 a week. Could you survive on that? No doubt there would be some buffering of retirees with very low incomes during the phasing out of the existing age-pension. Let's hope so for the Brownlows and the other millions this will affect.

The Millers have their super and money in managed funds. The weekly income they can generate independent of government pensions or subsidy is $552 – or around $276 in today's money. Could you survive on that? More important questions are, do you want to and will you have to? The choice is yours. You are responsible for your outcomes. You are in control of your future.

Starting your children on the road to wealth – without spending a cent!

When parents are asked what they would want for their children's future, most will say they want their children to be happy and secure.

"A is for 'assets', B is for 'banks', C is for 'compound interest' …"

163

Whilst we all know that by itself, money cannot make you happy, it can nevertheless help develop security and can create a buffer from worries that can erode happiness. What many parents do not realise is that they can help their children on the road to wealth at an early age and it will not cost them a cent!

There are many methods of wealth-building for children. Trust funds, savings accounts, education funds. All are worthy, all are helpful and all cost you, the parent, money! Whilst you yourselves are walking up the path to a financially independent retirement, it is possible for your children, once they are working, to do the same. If you let them 'borrow' the equity in the family home, they can get a headstart on the road and end up much further into wealth territory than we, at our age, could ever get. The young adults of today really do have time on their side! Instead of quoting that Oscar Wilde line that youth is wasted on the young, you can help them use their youth to generate a level of comfort and security in their later years.

Obviously, not all young people will be interested in working hard and saving for their 'distant' future, but many young people are suited to this path in their early adult years. You, the parent, are a good judge of the ability and commitment of your children. If they are interested in what you are doing with your investment plans, talk to them and explain that they too can achieve a life free of financial worry and dependence.

Lisa's story

Lisa is a good example of what can be achieved when there is a strong level of motivation and a model of sound investment practice is in place with the parents. Lisa came to me when she was 18. Her parents already had an investment property, which I had helped them to buy and were planning on buying another in four or five years' time. In the meantime, their actions had inspired Lisa. When she first came to see me, her parents owed around $100,000 on their family home in Berowra, in the north-west of Sydney. The home was worth $400,000. The investment property was worth $360,000 at that time. Their loan was $300,000. This meant that they had around $360,000 equity in the two properties.

I advised them to buy a property as 'tenants in common', so that the parents and Lisa were all named on the contract of ownership, but Lisa was named as owning 90 per cent and her parents only 10 per cent. This meant that the tax benefits came to Lisa, but the bank was legally satisfied that the property was also in the parents' names. By her 19th birthday, Lisa was the proud owner of her first investment property.

She bought a one-bedroom apartment 'off the plan' in Pyrmont, an inner city district of Sydney for $240,000. The principal and interest loan was for $260,000. Lisa was on $23,000 per annum, not exactly a huge income. The shortfall on the property, after all deductions and expenses, was around $90 a week to start with, since lower-income earners do not pay large amounts of tax and so cannot claim back so much tax in the first place. Lisa got a second job, two nights a week, to cover this shortfall.

Two years later, on her 21st birthday, Lisa was now in a new job, earning $33,000 a year. Her property was now worth $310,000! She had managed to reduce her debt to $240,000. She had already amassed $70,000 worth of equity in her own name! The rent on the apartment went up. Her deductions were higher because of her higher earnings. She was able to pay the debt off more quickly now.

By the end of 2002, Lisa will have reduced the debt further to $230,000. The value of her property will have increased to around $330,000. Her wages will also have increased. She will then purchase her second property! If she buys at around $330,000 and takes out another $350,000 loan, interest-only at first, by her 30th birthday her investment situation will look something like this if she sells the properties.

Property owned	approx.	$ 1,100,000
Loans outstanding	- approx.	$ 330,000
Capital gains tax and sales costs	- approx.	$ 208,000
Total profit	approx.	**$ 562,000**

Lisa hopes to be married and ready to start a family by the time she is 30. This money will be used for a large deposit to buy a house in Sydney and then she can start all over again! This time she will be able to use her own equity and, because of the large deposit she has put down on the house she buys for herself, she will be able to pay off the house in a few years and then pay off her next investment property, and the next, and the next ...

By the time Lisa retires she will be assured of a wealthy future. How much did this cost her parents? Nothing! What did it cost Lisa? For the first two years she took on two nights a week extra work. She didn't spend as much as her friends on clothes, going out to clubs and pubs and other entertainments, but she didn't stay home every night either! She kept a check on her spending and set her financial future as her priority in life. With life expectancies increasing, we will spend around 25 per cent of our lives retired. Lisa is guaranteed a lifestyle on retirement that many would envy. Her lifestyle before retirement will also benefit immensely from her commitment and financial intelligence. She will be able to buy her own home with a very large deposit, leaving her with very little debt and her own equity to continue her investment plans. Impressive!

Common questions

In my seminars I frequently get asked the same questions. Here are the most common ones in relation to residential property investment.

What about the possibility of a glut of properties and lack of tenants?

In deliberately choosing a property to attract a specific type of tenant you avoid the 'glut'. Most people who invest in residential property do not do the research we do and so buy the wrong property in the wrong place. By specialising you are buying in a smaller market. Not many people think that paying $350,000 for a one-bedroom apartment in the CBD is sensible. Only those who have done their homework understand where the demand is now falling in the rental market and what the tenants are looking for. Consequently there is no shortage of tenants either. I also recommend that you check out your property managers thoroughly to ensure they know what they are doing in regards to attracting the tenants you want.

With large developments, aren't the units all the same? Why will a tenant choose mine out of many?

The rents you charge for your premium properties should be realistic and should have been checked against the current market rents for similar properties. Overcharging on rent is both unnecessary and short-sighted. The premium properties you invest in are attractive for the appreciation of their capital value, not just the rent you can receive.

The tenants are fussy, so make sure whatever property you buy is beautifully finished and well-equipped. First impressions are the most powerful. Make sure the first impression your property gives is going to attract a potential tenant.

How will I cope with extended vacancies?

If you do your research and make sure that you have the right property at the right rent and the right property manager in place, there will be no extended vacancies. I normally advise investors to take out a slightly larger loan than they need so that they can pay for all the costs of buying the property from the loan and also so that they have a buffer against vacancies, should they ever need it. Very few do, but it's nice to know that, if the worst did happen, you could cover your interest repayments from the extra on your loan. All losses can of course be used later to reduce your tax bill in more profitable years.

What about interest rates. What are the chances they will reach 18 per cent again in the next 10 or 20 years?

Unfortunately I cannot predict the future. I'm not a gambling man either, which is reflected in my investment strategies. I prefer to play it safe wherever possible. By working out how much you can manage to borrow without starving or selling the children and then fixing the interest rates on your loans for five years or so, you are locking into a rate you can afford and can relax for that period. As that period comes to an end, say, six months before it finishes, have a look around. Can you afford to lock in again at the current rates on offer? If you are comfortable with your calculations, then lock in for another five years or so.

If the interest rates have suddenly shot up and you cannot afford the repayments anymore, then you have six months to find either a way to ride out the higher rates or to sell. Selling at this point is not recommended unless you really feel you have no choice. Selling a property when interest rates are very high is like selling shares because their value has fallen. You will not get the best possible price. If possible, hold on. These things are cyclic and what goes up will come down.

How do I know my investment value will keep growing at a high enough rate to sustain me in retirement?

By doing your homework and calculating how much you will need to retire on you will be able to calculate how much you need to invest in the first place with an estimated annual percentage of capital growth. I work out my figures with a conservative growth rate, currently around six per cent. I know my properties will actually achieve better than six per cent, but if the figures work on this percentage, think how wonderful you'll feel when you get more than you bargained for in capital growth!

Before you buy a property, you can check out the capital growth in the area through local real estate agents or by contacting the Real Estate Institute in your state. Obviously the previous figures are only an indicator to rates, but if the properties in the area have shown little or no capital growth in five years, they are probably not what you are looking for to make your investment work.

CHAPTER 12

FINAL WORDS

The most important part of any investment plan is, of course, YOU! Without the necessary financial intelligence behind it, even the most considered and well-researched plan will lead to nowhere. Whatever vehicle you select to carry your goals of financial independence and wealth, it will not go far without the right driver at the wheel. Rolls Royces crash as easily as Hyundais if the driver is incompetent.

It is important to be fully aware of barriers to wealth and independence that can exist in any of us. I may be repeating myself, but it's worthwhile to revisit the basic principles of behaviour and attitude that will govern your success or failure in any venture you choose to make.

The principles of successful investment

A well-defined purpose in life

Living your life without a clear idea of where you want to get to or what destination to make for is a waste of time and energy and about as effective as stumbling around in a strange maze in the dark. One of my friends works with teenagers. In the five years she has worked with them, not one of the hundreds she has talked to has any clear goal in life. Nearly all of them have said they want to be rich! When asked how they intend to achieve this, every young person but two said "Lotto!". The other two said stealing cars and robbing banks!

These young people were not unusual in their lack of clear and well-defined aims in life. Many young people at this stage in their lives have little or no idea of what they want beyond parties, money and a good time. What is more worrying is that there are many older people who have not grown past that stage and who still have no clear goals or purposes in life. It is this vagueness, this inability to make decisions or form an idea of the future that stops people from moving forward and causes them to live in a permanent fog, thinking no further than the next step, the next pay cheque, the next bill or the next month.

With a clear plan, right down to 'how much?', 'when by?' and 'how will I do this?' the fog disappears. The motivation to achieve is maintained when a definite purpose is kept in mind. The consequences of the goal you are headed for need to be held in your mind and played over again and again to keep up your motivation and purpose. A driving instructor once told me that the best way to steer a car is to look ahead, in front of you as far as you can – not down at the road immediately before you. The same applies to navigating your future.

Ambition

Linked to a well-defined purpose is ambition. Without ambition, it does not mean that a person has no goal. They may have a clear view of where they want to get to in their lives. Ambition, though, is the driving force, the fuel in the vehicle that enables it to cover the ground from here to there. Without ambition you cannot move. Being stuck is a frustrating and damaging place to be. It's like having a car bogged in a muddy ditch. If you cannot get it out, you cannot get to where you want to go, no matter how carefully you have planned the route to your destination. Without the ambition, the drive, and the three 'E's, energy, enthusiasm and effort, you will stay stuck in that ditch.

Ambition needs imagination and self-confidence. You need to be able to see yourself succeeding in your mind. If you can only imagine failure, guess what! That is what you will get. If you imagine yourself succeeding, time and time again, you will succeed. This is a proven psychological fact. Our elite sportsmen and women bear this out at every event they take part in.

Direction of effort

I was on my way to hosting a seminar in the country one summer. I had the air-conditioning on in the car and I also had the passenger-side window open a little to allow more ventilation. A fly flew in and battered its head against the driver's-side window for 20 minutes. It had a goal –

escape. It was giving 100 per cent total effort to reach its goal. It struck me that this fly had the right actions, the right effort and the right intentions of getting out of the car. All it had to do was look at the big picture, reassess the information and change directions.

How many people go through life doing exactly what the fly did? They have the right intentions, the right actions and the right amount of effort, but get no results. Without looking at the big picture, they will spend a lifetime banging their heads against a solid surface. Getting information and advice is necessary, because, like the fly, sometimes a change of direction or a change of tactic is necessary to achieve our goals and find the window that is already open to us.

Concentration of effort

Having mentioned 'effort', it is also necessary to look at the application of effort. Imagine you are watering a lawn. If you only apply water sporadically and only apply it to a few areas at a time, you will end up with a very patchy lawn. Some of it may look green and healthy. Other parts might be yellowing or bare. The big picture is not very pleasant. The big picture requires that you water the lawn – all of it – regularly. The big picture needs your energy, your effort and your enthusiasm to be maintained at a constant rate, not just every now and again, when you happen to feel like it!

For investment planning, you must spend time, effort and thought on all aspects of your plan and must do so in a consistent fashion, not just now and again. To go back to the garden analogy, each season needs different tasks to be accomplished at different times. Whilst some, like weeding, watering and protecting your plants need to be done all through the year, other tasks such as feeding, pruning, sowing, transplanting and harvesting need to be done at certain times of the year. Effort, energy and enthusiasm need to be applied in different ways, but they need to be present all year round for your garden or your investment plan to bear the fruit you want.

Persistence

Your plans may be sound, your heart and mind may be in the right place, the intention is there, but without persistence, you will not reach your goal.

Jake's story

Jake was a builder. He was a clever man with a good plan, but he did not persist and sold out his investments as soon as they had started to make a profit.

Many years ago he bought several cheap, rundown properties in Newtown, in Sydney's inner-west. At that time Newtown was fairly sleazy and very cheap. He bought these properties for around $20,000 and then renovated them. He did a great job. New kitchens, new bathrooms, new paint, new carpets. He inspired me to do the same. I bought my first property in Paddington in Sydney for $32,000 and proceeded to renovate. I then put it on the market 14 months later and it sold for $92,000. I used the profit to buy two more properties in Paddington and had them renovated. In 1985 I sold these properties and felt pretty pleased with myself when I made over $250,000 on them.

In 1997 I met Jake again. He had now retired, but did not feel he had enough income to live on in the way he wanted to live. He could not understand why all his hard work had not paid off. He had renovated and sold over 40 properties in Sydney's innner-west. He had sold many of these properties for a profit of around $10,000 to $20,000. The same properties were worth over $300,000 each in 1997! If he had held on to them and had supplemented his income with rent, rather than selling too soon to get immediate profit, he would be a multi-millionaire by now!

The two properties that I sold in Paddington are now worth over $600,000 each!

If only we had had the persistence and the clear vision at that time of our lives. Hopefully our mistakes will be useful to you on your journey to wealth. Buy assets and hold on to them! Imagine if your parents had bought an investment property when they were 40 and had held on to it. How much would it be worth now? How would their lives be different now? Sometimes we are so busy earning a living that we forget to consider the future. With a well-defined purpose, with the ambition and with persistence, Jake would have a very different experience of retirement today.

Getting the right information on financial matters

Without enough accurate information, no plan will work. Plans formed around guesswork or misinformation have a nasty habit of backfiring. Information is there for everyone to use. Go to the right people for the right information and use what they give you. A common source of misinformation is the 'expert' who works in a field related to but not directly involved in the field you want to research. Why go to a doctor if you have a toothache? Even a doctor would go to a dentist for that. A family law solicitor may be extremely helpful when it comes to divorce and child support, but is not the person you need when it comes to conveyancing. Your accountant may be the best accountant around, but when it comes to financial planning, wouldn't a financial planner be better?

Elisabeth's story

I met Elisabeth at a seminar in Sydney in 1996. She was recently divorced and her ex-husband's business had just gone bankrupt. At this time Elisabeth, a bright and resilient woman, wanted to take control of her financial future. She was 52 and worked in a job that paid her $38,000 a year. She had only been working there for a couple of years and was worried, rightly so, that she would not build up enough super to retire on comfortably. I calculated that she would have around $53,000 in super on retirement at 65. This would give her around $3,180 a year. Including the age pension, her total income would be around $350 a week on her eventual retirement. Not good news.

I suggested she buy an investment property and went through the figures with her to show her how it was possible and how much this would give her on retirement. The figure came to around $360,000 profit. Invested at 6 per cent, this would give her, along with her super of $53,000, an extra $24,870 a year, or around $480 a week to live on.

Elisabeth was happy with this but wanted to check the figures with her accountant. I warned her that the accountant was not an expert on financial planning and she might be better off finding an independent financial planner to go through the figures. Unfortunately she did not heed this advice and came back to me a week later saying that her accountant had told her that shares were the way to go and she was going to follow his advice. She borrowed $50,000 and bought a share portfolio through a managed fund that cited around 8 per cent average yearly return, historically.

By the time she wanted to retire, this managed fund investment would be worth around $150,000. After paying back the loan and paying capital gains tax when she moved the money to a different fund, more appropriate for her retirement, she would be left with around $80,000 in profit. Add this to her super and the total investment would be $133,000. This would give her nearly $8,000 a year. This is $17,000 LESS than the outcome from property investment. I pointed this out to her, but she seemed to think that, because he was an accountant, he should know what he was talking about! Ouch! The thought of this one still hurts!

Practising self-discipline

The meaning of the word 'discipline' has more to do with teaching than punishment. We tend to forget this. Most of us associate the concept of self-discipline with the idea of giving up something and missing it afterwards or making ourselves do something we don't really want to do. We don't want to stop buying things or eating chocolate biscuits. We don't want to feel the discomfort of giving up our destructive and wasteful habits. If it means we have to make an effort to do something, many of us are too lazy to do this and continue our bad habits regardless of the consequences.

"But I'm only having one!"

The carrot on the stick must be bigger than the carrot immediately in front of us to make us move forward. The desire to reach a goal may be strong, but, without having a concrete result in mind, the desire may become overwhelmed by apathy, laziness or procrastination.

Our faith in our ability to achieve our goals has to be strong enough. Our goals need to be dangling right in front of us every day for us to learn to change our habits. We need the self-esteem and confidence in ourselves to believe we can make a difference in our own futures and change damaging habits into constructive habits. We need to unlearn some habits and learn others. This is the essence of self-discipline, teaching ourselves to function more effectively and live more constructively. Self-esteem goes hand in hand with this, since it gives us a sense of being worth such efforts, of being worthy of wealth and success.

The habit of indiscriminate spending is a consequence of the lack of self-discipline. Write down all that you spend each day for a month. Separate out all the necessities, such as bills, transport costs, necessary groceries (I do not class chocolate bars, cosmetics, cigarettes or alcohol as necessities!) and mortgage repayments. Add up the rest and multiply it by 12. This is how much you are wasting each year. Now work out how long you have until retirement. Let's say you have 25 years to go and you waste $6,000 a year. That is $150,000 you could have saved! This task will bring home clearly how damaging the lack of self-discipline and lack of self-awareness can be to your future.

Paul and Anika

Paul and Anika are an example of a lack of self-discipline leading to destructive habits. Between them they earned $200,000 a year. Their home was worth around $550,000. They still owed $220,000 on it and could only afford to pay off $15,000 a year, just covering the interest. Where was their money going? They both leased cars to the tune of $20,000 a year! They went on expensive holidays, costing around $15,000 a year. They spent $1,000 or so a month on entertainment. They paid nearly $1,000 a month on their credit cards' interest alone! When I talked to them about cutting back, they looked horrified! What would their friends think? They did say they would think about it and would get back to me. That was six years ago. Luckily I didn't hold my breath!

Overcoming procrastination, fear and over-caution

Many years ago the neighbours of some friends of mine had a family tragedy that made them look at their lives in a very different way. Their three-year old son drowned in a backyard swimming pool. They were in the backyard, 10 metres away, when he died. It was a silent and quick death. The real tragedy was that it was preventable. They had planned to take him to swimming lessons and had been talking about it for 12 months, but they had never got around to it. They were always too busy, or would put it off for another month. After all, there seemed to be no

175

urgency. It could wait until he got a bit older. He never did get older.

Since that day, they have lost the habit of procrastination. Everything is done immediately. Every plan is acted on as if there is no tomorrow. For all you know, tomorrow may never come. Procrastination is a killer. Act now. Putting things off kills growth and progress.

Stefan and Anna

Stefan and Anna decided that after they were married they were going to invest in property – to speed up their investment plans and create a large deposit for the house they wanted to buy for themselves. They found a unit for $130,000 in Maroubra, a Sydney beach suburb. Their friends suggested they go on an expensive honeymoon, buy a new car and enjoy themselves whilst they were still young. After all things would not change that much over just a few years. They decided to wait a while. They bought a car. They had a nice honeymoon. A few years wouldn't make much difference, would it?

Six years later they decided to look again. The average unit price had gone beyond $210,000. They had continued to save, but the prices had risen faster than they could save. The unit they had first looked at was now worth $220,000. When they came to me, I was able to help them invest in property, but they had basically wasted six years of their life and thousands of dollars through procrastination and taking the advice of people who knew nothing about investment.

Fear is often behind procrastination. Laziness can be another factor, but fear and over-caution are the main factors, at least in the cases I have encountered. Caution has its place in investment planning, but fear and over-caution are destructive. Information from qualified and experienced people is the best cure for fear. Do the research, do your homework, add up the figures, talk to the bank and then DO IT! Procrastination gets you nowhere. Keep that clear, concrete picture of your goal in front of you. Find a picture or image that represents it and keep it where you can look at it every day. Every day do just one small thing that takes you closer to your goal. It could be saving a few dollars by not buying that piece of cake after lunch. It could be walking into a bank and picking up some literature on what investment funds they manage. It could be looking up a method of investment on the internet. It could be making a telephone call to your super fund to find out what options are available for more profitable returns on your long-term super investment. It could be something as simple as adding a few details to the mental picture of how you want your life to be after retirement. All these actions, though small, prevent procrastination and help to allay fears.

Defining our concept of wealth

Everyone has his or her own idea of what it means to be wealthy. Carl, who I mentioned at the beginning of the book, wanted peace, tranquility, and the freedom to do what he wanted. He gained that and maintains it on $150 a week.

I have a different version of wealth that costs a lot more! Whatever your definition is, work it out and cost it. Then you will know when what you have is enough. It will also mean a clearer goal and will make it easier to get there.

Remember the words of Buckminster Fuller,

"I am wealthy when I have an income stream that will generate enough money to live the lifestyle I desire before I get out of bed in the morning."

Whatever you do, do something!

The most expensive course of action is to do nothing. The government can make no promises that they will support you in your retirement. Today's age pension is only a means to survive, not to live by. The trend towards self-funded retirement is no accident. It is being encouraged by governments around the world, because they know that current population trends will lead to increased spending on the support and welfare of an ageing population and they do not know how they will fund this spending. If you do not help yourself into your future, there will be very little future left for you.

Your future is in your control. With financial intelligence, you can make it a secure and satisfying future, free of financial worry and struggle. The one thing you must do is START NOW! Make your plans and then put them into action. Get the right advice. Put into place some good habits. Keep a goal clear in your mind and stay focused on achieving it.

If there are people around you who are, through their own fears or laziness, willing to undermine your future, develop a thick skin, ignore them and keeping moving towards your future. You will find they get left behind. Be persistent, be patient and believe in your ability to change your life.

In the words of the immortal Dr Seuss in *Oh, the Places You'll Go!*

"And will you succeed?
Yes! You will, indeed!
(98 and ¾ per cent guaranteed.)

KID, YOU'LL MOVE MOUNTAINS!

So...
Be your name Buxbaum or Bixby or Bray
Or Mordecai Ali Van Allen O'Shea,
You're off to Great Places!
Today is your day!
Your mountain is waiting.

So... *get on your way!"*

Useful contacts

Real Estate Investors Network (REIN)
Level 9, 2 Bligh Street, Sydney, NSW 2000
Postal address: GPO Box 160, Sydney, NSW 2001
Phone: 1800 001 003
Fax: 1800 002 303
Web: www.rein.com.au

Australian Securities and Investments Commission (ASIC)
ASIC Infoline: 1300 300 630
Web: http://www.asic.gov.au

Australian Stock Exchange (ASX)
Phone: (02) 9227 0000
Web: www.asx.com.au

Australian Taxation Office (ATO)
Refunds, lodgements and Tax File numbers: 13 28 63
Info for Older Australians: 13 28 62
Personal tax enquiries: 13 28 61
Superannuation helpline: 13 10 20
Web: General www.ato.gov.au

Association of Superannuation Funds of Australia (ASFA)
Phone: (02) 9264 9300
Web: www.superannuation.asn.au

Financial Planning Association of Australia Ltd (FPA)
Phone: 1800 626 393
Web: www.fpa.asn.au

Cannex
For current interest rates for loans from financial institutions
Web: www.cannex.com.au

Real Estate Institute of Australia (REIA)
Phone: (02) 6282 4277
Web: www.reia.asn.au

Recommended reading

Rather than give you a long list of worthwhile books, I have chosen to list a few of my personal favourites. Some have inspired me. Some have been excellent sources of information. Many are available through libraries and all are available from Australian bookshops.

George S. Clason – "The Richest Man In Babylon"

Napoleon Hill – "Think And Grow Rich"

Robert Kiyosaki – "Rich Dad, Poor Dad"

Noel Whittaker – "Making Money Made Simple" and other titles

Paul Clitheroe – "The Road To Wealth"

Peter Switzer – "Busting Debt" and other titles

Bernard Salt – "The Big Shift"

John McGrath – "You Don't Have To Be Born Brilliant"